THIS IS THE
BASSET HOUND

THIS IS THE
BASSET HOUND

by

Ernest H. Hart

Distributed in the U.S.A. by T.F.H. Publications, Inc., 211 West Sylvania Avenue, P.O. Box 27, Neptune City, N.J. 07753; in England by T.F.H. (Gt. Britain) Ltd., 13 Nutley Lane, Reigate, Surrey; in Canada to the book store and library trade by Clarke, Irwin & Company, Clarwin House, 791 St. Clair Avenue West, Toronto 10, Ontario; in Canada to the pet trade by Rolf C. Hagen Ltd., 3225 Sartelon Street, Montreal 382, Quebec; in Southeast Asia by Y.W. Ong, 9 Lorong 36 Geylang, Singapore 14; in Australia and the south Pacific by Pet Imports Pty. Ltd., P.O. Box 149, Brookvale 2100, N.S.W., Australia. Published by T.F.H. Publications, Inc. Ltd., The British Crown Colony of Hong Kong.

to
Stephanie Alexandra
and
Allan Mathew

photographs by: Gilbert, Dean, Brown, Schley, Shafer, Ludwig, Three Lions, Inc., Tauskey, Dodds, Gilmore, Streeter, Van der Meid, and special thanks to Dr. Leonard Skolnik, owner of Slippery Hill Kennels, for his ready cooperation which so greatly enhanced the pictorial value of this book. line drawings and book design by the author

THIS IS THE
BASSET HOUND

Contents

Ch. Santana Mandeville's Gigolo by Ch. Santana
Count Dracula x Ch. Phoebe of Mandeville
Breeder-owner, Santana-Mandeville Basset
Kennels
Mr. and Mrs. Paul E. Nelson

CHAPTER I

Origin of the Basset Hound

To search out the origin of the Basset Hound one must go beyond the breed as we know it today, or in the recent yesterdays, and find the hidden roots from which grew this hound that has captured our interest. Before, then, we can find the basic origin of this one specific family we must first know more about the species canine, of which our breed is a section, so that we can more fully appreciate the processes of evolution, selection, and environment; the natural tools that nature has given to us with which to fashion a breed and change or mold it to fit our purpose.

In a time so long ago that it defies the human mind, approximately forty million years, the canine species began to develop on an earth itself not yet stable. The reptilian monsters, the giants of great size and fantastic and fearful mien that had roamed this plastic, forming earth for so long that it seemed that they would never cease to be, were too limited in genetic scope, mentally and physically, and could not mutate or change to meet and exist in a changing environment. From the north came the first of the several ice ages that covered the earth with a frozen crust and the herbivorous dinosaurs did not have intelligence enough to attempt to find forage beneath the cap of snow. The hideous tear-toothed reptilian carnivores were slowed by the cold, with which they couldn't cope, to a dying stagger, and these horrendous kings of the Earth were swept away by the eons-long phases of the ice age.

But during the almost unending Mesozoic era that had echoed to the roars of these giants as they ate and shivered themselves into oblivion, dramatic mutations occurred within the germ plasm of some of the smaller, lesser reptilian creatures as nature clumsily experimented with what was at hand in a desperate attempt to perpetuate animal life forms on our planet.

Various changes took place, slowly, laboriously in a tentative groping for life that could accept and mutate with change. The genetic formulas of these smallish, living creatures had to become more complicated and varied as well as elastic to hold the secret seeds of change so that life could go on under varied environment. Skeletal changes took place, body scales changed to fur and feathers; some reptiles displayed greater energy than their generally slower moving, almost brainless kin and certain others began to develop warm blood to heat the body against cold. The seat of greater reaction to stimuli shifted from the spinal ganglia to the brain, animals grew smaller and so able to sustain themselves and reproduce on much less food, and the intake ability of a greater variety of nutritional elements became incorporated in the genetic scheme of these creatures. The proportions, as well as size, of this living mass of transitional forms began to change. The resulting creatures, after this yeasty stirring and selection, were the precursors of the various animal families that would solidify and take shape and substance upon the earth, most important of all being the forming mammalian, viviparous, hair-bearing, milk-producing, intelligent creatures that were destined to become the dominant life forms of this world and which were to eventually include the two creatures in which we are particularly interested—mankind and the Basset Hound.

During the Paleocene age mammalian carnivores began to reach definition as animal entities. The eons rolled away into infinity and, living furtively in the primaeval forests, a very inconspicuous part of the teeming, awesome animal population of a still humanless earth, during the twenty million or so years of the Eocene period that followed the mammals began to quietly segregate and specialize. And, during those millions of years of stretched and painful genesis, there finally appeared, along with rodents and cat-creatures, the dog-like mammal labeled *Mesonyx*.

During the Oligocene period many of the mammals, like the earlier reptilian monsters, became victims of their own organic simplicity and became extinct but, in the evolving and multiplying gene-pool of the primitive flesh eaters, small and beneficial mutations occurred that gave rise to new sub-species within the already wide carnivorous evolutionary format. Those that were more capable of adapting to environmental change to compete in their habitat continued to flourish, and from these vigorous and more plastic species came the two great modern groups of meat-eaters, emerging gradually into the light of recognition; the solitary, stalking cats and the canines who specialized in the pack pursuit of their quarry.

Miacis, the ancestor of the canine family who lived forty million years ago, was a strange looking creature; small, furtive, arboreal, and probably nocturnal, he looked more like a weasel but was the ancestor of the dogs, bears and similar creatures. Miacis lived long before the curious simian creature that was the ancestor of man crept from the sheltering tree limbs down to the forest floor and found the path to social consciousness.

10

The first true canine, *Tomarctus*, was long and low to the ground and sported a heavy long tail. *Tomarctus* was the prototype dog that was the direct ancestor of the family *Canidae* that included wolves, foxes, coyotes and jackals.

As the varied hosts of animal life moved sluggishly toward their diverse evolutionary paths a descendant of Miacis, known as *Cynodictus*, gave tremendous impetus to numerous mammalian families through his genetic formula. He is known as the grandfather of the canine family and, though not yet a true canine, there came from Cynodictus many mammalian families that eventually, in the crucible of the ages, took form as bears, cats, raccoons, hyenas, wolves, and seals. Finally, a product of random selection from this varied stock, there emerged the true father of the family canine, the prototype dog, *Tomarctus*. A short-legged, long bodied, long-tailed predator, Tomarctus roamed the earth about fifteen million years ago and was the direct ancestor of wolves, coyotes, jackals, foxes and dogs.

Directly descending from Tomarctus, during the Miocene era, and the most important cleavage in canine genealogy, there appeared on the scene the four prototype breeds of canine from which came, in a rough form, all our breeds of dogs; *Canis familiaris metris-optimae*, *Canis familiaris intermedius*, *Canis familiaris leineri* and *Canis familiaris inostranzewi*. From metris-optimae came the sheep-herding breeds; from intermedius, working and hunting dogs; from leineri, hounds and later terriers, and from inostranzewi, heavy-jawed fighting dogs and some retrievers.

These categories are necessarily broad in concept because many of the breeds we know today are the result of an intermingling of the heritage of animals that descended from the four basic types named above. But all the many breeds, in all their varied physical aspects, are one and the same

11

species. The bewildering diversity of sizes, shapes and abilities are evidence of the touch of man.

Nature, through millions of years of evolution, finally produced the above mentioned four major prototypes for the fashioning of the canine race. Man then came into the picture and molded the species canine to his own wants, controlling the evolutionary process of the dog through selection and, in the near past, the present and, we hope, the future, through clever manipulation of canine germ-plasm.

What has been written so far has no direct application to the Basset Hound except in a general sense. Ancient history never does seem to have any but a remote affiliation with the present but, in its own right, has interest and a thread smacking of the romance of ancient heritage that intrigues many of us. I think that what you have read here, briefly, of the beginning and progression of the canine race has that smattering of romance and interest and now leads us directly to the specific origin of the Basset Hound.

As the name indicates, the Basset is a hound, and to have developed breeds of dogs as hounds or hunting dogs, it follows that there had to have been hunters and this occupation was the earliest known vocation of mankind. Therefore hunting dogs were the first kind of dogs used in any direct capacity by early man. First the dog followed man on the hunt. Then, when man recognized the superior scenting and hearing ability of

Ch. Peg O' My Heart of Greenly Hall
The Greenly Hall Basset Kennel developed the desired front specified by the present standard in the 1940's, well before anyone else. The shoulder layback and sternum are as good or better than found on today's show dogs.

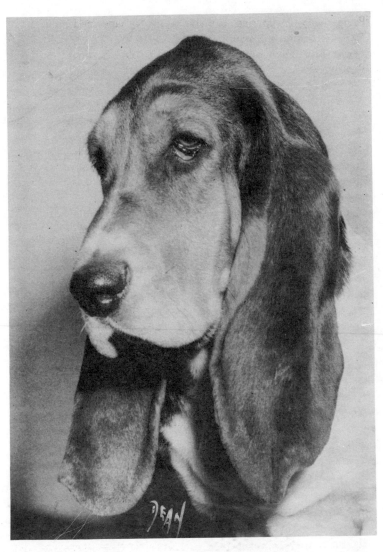

Headstudy of Ch. Gwendolyn of Mandeville, a
top producing Basset bitch, exhibiting the type
and classic elegance called for in the breed
standard. Breeders, owners, handlers:
Mr. and Mrs. Paul E. Nelson.

Ch. Duke of Greenly Hall
This photograph was taken in the 1930's. Duke
was the basic or root sire of a famous bloodline.
The breeders of this great family improved type
through a well-managed breeding program.
Most of our modern Bassets show genetic
relationship to this source.

the dog, he allowed the dog to lead the hunt. Subsequently when man realized that certain animals were better hunters than others he selected from their progeny and for their specific type and, in so doing, took the first giant step toward the manipulation of animal evolution and specifically the breeding of dogs for special tasks.

The destinies of dog and man seem to have ever run parallel. In those early times they complemented each other. The dog's natural talents aided man in supplying food and furs for his family. It was fleet where man was slow; it had a highly developed scenting ability and its hearing was many times sharper than man's. To pay his canine companion for its help in hunting, in warning of danger and in keeping the dangerous carnivores from the cave door, man gave the dog shelter, food, affection, and tended his injuries.

Gradually from the mass of hunting breeds developed by man in various parts of the world, two different types came into focus; the long-

Ch. Kelly's Chief Hareman
Famous in the 1940's, this prepotent stud made
his championship in 1941 and was the progenitor
of the Belbay Kennels. He was grandsire of the
Belbay stalwarts Triumph, Treasure, and Design.
The name of this important male can be found in
the pedigrees of most present-day dogs.

eared hounds that took scent from the ground and trailed the quarry, and the long-legged, swift gaze-hounds that utilized their highly developed sighting ability to see the game and subsequently to run it down through their speed of foot. This latter type of hunting dog became the vogue in Egypt, land of the pyramid and cradle of human history. There the Egyptian Greyhound was brought to full fruition and became the progenitor, along with the Saluki and the Afghan, both of similar type, of the several races of sight or gaze-hounds, animals still used for the same purpose today as they were in that long ago time of the Pharaohs.

Written accounts inform us of the great ability of the Greeks as dog breeders; 2400 years ago Xenophon, in his *Cynegeticus*, instructs us in the correct handling of hounds. We know also that, about 500 B.C., crosses between the hound type dogs (those that used their scenting ability to follow a trail) and the Mastiff type descended from *Canis familiaris inostranzewi* were interbred to produce hounds of larger size that could

15

Ch. Gladstone of Mandeville
by Ch. Huey of Cypress x Ch. Hamlin's Missie
Breeder-owner: Santana-Mandeville Basset
Kennels.

be used to hunt bigger and more ferocious game. Genetically, we know now, such crosses would give tongue, or bay, when trailing. From these latter crosses, after many generations and much selection and refinement, came the ancestors of the St. Hubertus Brachen or St. Hubert Hounds which were the direct ancestor of the Basset Hound.

The great Norman Hounds of St. Hubert, their name taken from that of the famous Bishop of Liege, who lived in the early part of the eighth century, mirrored the eye for a dog and the sporting quality of the Bishop. He had a passion for a good hound and for hunting, and reveled in the belling voice of a good-baying hound on a hot trail. These great St. Hubertus Brachen breed of hounds became the fountainhead from which flowed other great hound breeds; the Bloodhound, Talbot Hound, Vendee Hound, and Basset Hound, to name a few. As a matter of fact Professor Lutz Heck, a well known scientist and director of the Berlin Zoo, named the Brachen as the master strain of hunting dogs from which all other forms descended.

Selection was made for shorter leg length and lower station, aided by canny use of mutations from the norm toward this wanted anatomical feature and soon the breed was established and found to be especially useful in hunting the European hare. Since the Abbots of St. Hubert annually contributed a number of hounds to the King's kennels as a part of the tax which they were forced to pay the monarchy, the short-legged Basset Hound soon found itself used in the royal hunt and its popularity as a hunting dog became, with royal patronage, firmly established.

The Normans were great hunters and their esteem of the short-legged breed gave it importance. They, the Normans, used the breed much as the Spaniel was used in Spain, England, and America. But the extremely keen scent of the breed (which was only rivaled by the scenting powers of the Bloodhound) gave the Basset a wider latitude and, instead of using these hounds exclusively on small game, many hunters used them to track boar, wolf, deer and other large game. Larger, fiercer dogs were kept leashed and then loosed upon the quarry after the Basset pack had tracked it to its lair. The fact that the Basset seemed to have a more natural inclination to retrieve than most hounds made the breed valuable on birds. Today, in this country and abroad, Bassets are often used on birds, particularly pheasant, as well as rabbit and hare.

Due to the presence of the great St. Hubertus Brachen, many valuable hound breeds were developed in France, but the records of the crosses that produced them were never kept or, if they were, have been lost in the ages. It is entirely feasible that the Bloodhound and the Talbot Hound were merged to produce the Basset Hound and a mutation for short legs occurred in the subsequent stock and was favored and selected for. In appearance, as we can see, the Basset very closely resembles the Blood-hound while from the Talbot Hound could have come the open, black, tan and white markings; the Talbot Hound was the direct ancestor of the Foxhound who bears this coloring and markings from its ancestral source. There could also have been a cross to the Vendee Hound, ancestor of the Otterhound, and this could account for the wire or rough-coated variety of Basset Hounds. Subsequent crosses back to the St. Hubert strain would have strengthened and given added finish to the basic strain.

In Eastern France and later in Germany a strain of Bassets were developed that were black and tan in color and marked like a Doberman. They were not at all uncommon in these areas and were noted for their marvelous scenting and staying powers. It is not impossible to believe that these early Bassets of black and tan coloration that were imported to Germany were the basis, combined with an early German terrier breed, of the Dachshund.

The word "basset" means "low-set," and the breed certainly fits this description, but most of the earlier specimens were not nearly as low to the ground as those we see in the show ring today. They were low-set enough for their size to earn their name and, as time passed and breeders exaggerated the shortness of limbs the breed developed an uncanny persistence and perseverance in the field, even greater than that of most hounds. This exaggeration of certain characteristics, in this case to the point where instead of perseverance and persistence stubborness could be substituted as being more descriptive, was directly associated with the gradual shortening of leg-length, for without these characteristics the short-legged Basset could never push and scramble through the brambles and brush of the hunting field and would finally give up before the game was cornered. But with these characteristics a part of the temperament and mental quality of the breed, our stout, short-legged Basset Hounds are always gamely there at the finish.

Ichabod at ten months of age. Even at this young age he exhibits the correct and wanted head shape for a male Basset. This youngster is the epitome of quality.

CHAPTER II

History of the Basset Hound

In France, where the Basset originated, the breed was also called the Artesian Basset and the Artois Dog or *Chien d'Artois*. The latter name was also used to designate the large hounds of Picardy, so the short-legged hounds in which we are interested were called Bassets to distinguish them from the Chiens d'Artois, the Picardy strain of hunting hounds.

The earliest Basset Hounds sported two qualities in coat; the smooth coated and the rough coated. The smooths were bred throughout Artois with the finest of the smooth coated strains coming from the vicinity of Vendée. The breeders from Flanders seemed to be partial to the rough coated variety and they were bred extensively in this area. These rough coated (or Basset Grifon) dogs, in the earlier strains, carried coats that were very similar to the Otterhound in both coat color and texture. They were known for their courage, of which they seemed to possess an overabundance. They were exceedingly stubborn and their temperament was not as even and dependable as their contemporary smooth-coated brethren (seemingly a correlation between coat quality and difference in temperament), and were therefore much less desirable as pets and house dogs than the smooth coated animals. These Basset Grifons were, nevertheless, well liked by sportsmen who kept them kenneled and used them in the field for their staunchness and courage, two attributes that are certainly to be wished for in a hunting dog of any type.

Both the smooth coated and the rough coated strains were divided into three major classes; 1. the crooked-legged Basset (*Basset à jambes tortues*) 2. the half-crooked-legged Basset (*Basset à jambes demi-tortues*) 3. the straight-legged Basset (*Basset à jambes droites*).

The crooked-legged Basset was heavy in bone, houndy and very typical; rather a slight exaggeration in basic type; a powerful, strong animal with a good clear voice on trail. The half-crooked legged Basset was lighter in bone than the full crooked-legged dogs bred before the turn of the century in about 1890, and the straight-legged Bassets were still lighter in bone and substance than the other two, and they were the fastest afoot of the three

21

varieties. In type the straight-legged Basset, in that early time, looked somewhat like a houndier, longer-bodied and slightly shorter-legged English Beagle.

The man to whom Basset breeders owe a good deal was the Count le Couteult* de Canteleu. He was one of the few French noblemen of his day (the last half of the nineteenth century) who, living the life of a grand-seigneur on his magnificent estate, went to great trouble and expense to collect every particle of information obtainable about this breed he loved. He traced the history of the breed after long years of study and winnowing out small bits of information and putting them together in proper sequence, much as we have here on these pages, and he justly took a patriotic pride in obtaining the best specimens that could be found in France and breeding from them. Through his enthusiasm, his ability and his name, combined with his legendary sportsmanship, he succeeded in again establishing the Basset Hound in public favor. The Le Couteult strain of Bassets, from the kennels and of the breeding of the Count, is one of the two modern strains of Bassets popular in France.

The second strain of popular Bassets of recent years is the Lane strain, established by Mons. Lane of Francquevilli, near Boos. The difference between the two strains lies mostly in head properties, the Lane strain possessing a broad and rather coarse skull and a large, round eye quite similar to the eye of the Beagle. The head of the Le Couteult strain is breedier in appearance and narrower, similar to a fine quality Bloodhound bitch's head proportions. The eye is dark brown, sunken in folds of flesh with a prominent (typically Bloodhound) haw. The cheeks are flat, in comparison to the sides of the Lane strain heads which have well developed cheeks. The whole head is narrow and downfaced and has a look of unutterable sadness and patience. This, the Le Couteult strain Basset is the type favored by breeders and the show fancy in England and America.

Other points in which the two strains differed was in size, the Lane hound being slightly larger. This same strain were, along with greater size, very strong and heavy dogs, more crooked in foreleg and not as rich in coat color or as silky in coat quality as the Le Couteult hounds. The basic Lane hounds were lemon and white or pale tan and white and occasionally roan. Both strains were, in the best specimens, fine animals. By judicious merging of the genetic qualities of both strains and rigid selection for specific type, the strong, beautiful, breedy Basset Hound of today was fashioned.

In France the Vendeen, or Basset Grifon, is still popular and visitors to

Author's note: The name Couteult is sometimes also spelled Couteulx. Here we have anglicized the name in part. In French it would be Le Comte le Couteult de Canteleu.

Ch. Hartshead Pepper
A well known dog of the past, bred by Emil and
Effie Slitz, who are still active and have been
interested in the breed for almost forty-five
years. Pepper won at Westminster '48 and '49.

that country will still see these attractive, rough-coated Basset Hounds in
many areas still being bred by a good many well-known fanciers. Frequently at shows in France one will see more of the rough-coated variety
benched than the smooth type which is so popular here. In France also
was bred the Blue Gascon, a mottled blue-colored hound, sometimes at
an extreme, marked with the white background and black splotches of a
Harlequin Great Dane but with tan thumb-marks above the eyes. The blue
phase is much like a merle and I suspect has the same kind of color inheritance. There are also the Black and Tans of Ardennes district that are
marked like a Doberman Pinscher or a Dachshund. These latter colored
dogs are also prone to throw solid reds in litters. The various strains and
color varieties of Basset Hounds have been, in the past, so often crossed

to give to one strain what was valuable in another, that even today recessives that have been carried in the genetic formula for many, many generations will occasionally, in a specific breeding, meet like recessives and we find odd colors or changes in type in one or two of the whelps in the nest; genetic echoes haunting us from the past.

THE BASSET HOUND IN ENGLAND

*The first Basset Hounds to be imported to England were sent by the Count de Tournow to Lord Galway in 1866. They were a nice, matched pair and Lord Galway christened them Basset and Belle. The following year this pair produced a litter for Lord Galway, the first litter of Bassets bred in England. These animals were subsequently sold to Lord Onslow in 1872 when their previous owner lost interest in the breed. From the kennels of the Count le Couteult de Canteleu the kennels of Lord Onslow received some fine stock to augment his pack along with the animals purchased from Lord Galway.

The history of the breed as a show dog in England began in 1874, when Sir Everett Millais saw a Basset Hound in the collection at the Jardin d'Acclimation in Paris. Inquiry revealed the fact that this breed that took his fancy was an established one that had been used for many generations by French sportsmen in the field and bred completely true. Millais bought and brought back to England with him a Basset Hound named Model. This dog was shown at Wolverhampton, the first of the breed ever benched and shown in England, all former imports having been owned by sportsmen and used only in the field.

Lord Onslow, mentioned earlier, sold his pack in 1882 consisting of fifteen splendid pairs of hounds to Sir Everett Millais and George Krehl, and it was from these basic animals that the finest Bassets in England and America are descended though, as we shall see, the Basset in America was a much earlier arrival than he was even in England. Sir Everett wrote a good description of the breed calling them "small running hounds" (*petit chiens courant*) which confused breeders of the day interested in tracing the ancestry of their Basset Hounds with accuracy. Mr. Krehl, a man of conviction and energy, did much for the success and popularity of the breed in England. Later, Sir Everett Millais, due to ill health, was forced to withdraw his interest and activity in behalf of the Basset Hound and, almost simultaneously, Lord Onslow broke up his pack.

Luckily such a man as George Krehl still held high the banner of the breed, and it was through his efforts that the popularity of the short-

Author's note: History records that James IV, of Scotland, used Bassets to find and rout game into the open for his Greyhounds to sight and pursue.

legged French canine immigrant grew. He it was who kept the breeders in touch with each other and lent them of his own enthusiasm and finally, in February 1883, largely through his efforts, a meeting of the leading Basset breeders in England took place at 25 Downing Street to form a Basset Hound Club and encourage, through the club, the breeding of Basset Hounds for exhibition and hunting.

The following members were enrolled: G. R. Krehl, D. C. Crake, Mr. Blaine, Mr. Munro, H. B. Watson, W. P. Alleyne, H. Wyndham Carter, G. Barton, C. Collett, H. Blackett, E. Durant, A. Masson, C. Blackburne, and A. Krehl. The elected president was Count le Couteult de Canteleu, and the vice-presidents were Lord Onslow and G. R. Krehl; the latter gentleman was also named treasurer. H. W. Carter was elected secretary, and the Board of Governors consisted of W. P. Alleyne, E. Durant, H. B. Watson, G. R. Krehl, and H. W. Carter.

The club formed a pack for hunting that was kenneled at Maidenhead. Mr. Alleyne, elected Huntsman, gave permission for the pack to use his kennels in Maidenhead.

At about this time canny Mr. Krehl, well knowing the importance of royal patronage, presented a brace of puppies sired by his fine stud, Jupiter, to H.R.H. the Prince of Wales. Intrigued by the "quaintness" of the puppies His Royal Highness expressed his delight in the new additions to his kennels by presenting Mr. Krehl with a scarf pin in the design of the Prince's Plumes. His Royal Highness made use of his Bassets for rabbit shooting in Scotland. English breeders began to import some of the better, rough-coated specimens from France and these too, found favor in the Royal Kennels for many years and fine specimens of the rough-coated Basset Hound were exhibited with much pride by the Prince of Wales.

Most of the Bassets imported into England and up to the time (and beyond) of the formation of the Basset Hound Club of England were brought in and subsequently bred by sportsmen and used exclusively in the field. The largest exhibition of stock on the show bench was made by Sir Everett Millais at the Wolverhampton show in 1880. The size of the entry guaranteed notice by the dog fancy, and the breed certainly did attract attention. But following this one bid for popularity entries at the shows were very small and often not one specimen of the breed was to be found on the benches. Good Bassets were not easy to breed, even from the fine imported stock available at the time, and top show specimens

Author's note: In a city museum in Quito, Ecuador, the author found two paintings of typey French Bassets by Petit, 19th century French painter. One was of smooths, the other roughs.

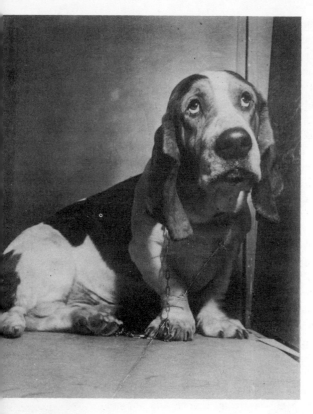

Ch. Promise of Greenly Hall as a puppy in 1940. When bred to Ch. Duchess of Greenly Hall he produced Ch. Maitri of Lyn Mar Acres, root brood bitch of the famous Lyn Mar Kennels. A host of other top producing get also resulted from this breeding.

were few and far between. As a result, except at the very largest shows in England, the Basset Hound was relegated to the variety classes and given no breed classes of its own.

THE BASSET HOUND IN AMERICA

The earliest Basset Hounds that can be found mentioned on our soil were sent to George Washington by his good friend and fellow-in-arms, Lafayette. No less an authority than George Washington himself is the source for this information, for it is written by him in his voluminous diary that Basset Hounds were sent by his friend from France to these shores after the Revolutionary War. Other Bassets probably came accompanying their masters from England and France, but of them we have no records. We do know that there was a breed of rabbit hound called the "Old Virginian Bench-Legged Beagle" that could very well have been the product of outcrossing Basset Hounds to Beagles, the latter hound having been a very popular breed in those days and, for that matter, still.

26

Ch. Mon Philippe of Greenly Hall, one of the greatest producing sires of the famous Greenly Hall bloodlines. This dog's genetic worth had a marked influence on the breed in the 1950's. Note the quality he displays in the photo.

There was a brace of Basset Hounds brought by Lord Aylesford to his ranch near Big Springs, Texas, where they were used as rabbit hounds. These Texas Bassets were sired by Mr. G. R. Krehl's Jupiter, the same stud who sired the Basset puppies given to H.R.H. the Prince of Wales. Then, in 1883, a Mr. Chamberlain purchased a fine open marked Basset Hound named Nemours from Mr. Krehl and brought him to America and to the Maizeland Kennels. At the Westminster Kennel Club Show, the following spring (1884), Nemours was entered and the Basset Hound made his debut in the American show ring. The following year Mr. Gilbert, of New Haven, Connecticut, imported Bertrand, sired by Bourbon, and Canace, sired by Mr. Krehl's fertile Jupiter.

In this same year, 1885, the American Kennel Club registered its first Basset Hound, Bouncer, owned by Collin Cameron of Bickerville, Pa. This dog is listed as having been bred by Pottinger Dorsey of New Market, Va., whelped March 1881; a black, tan and white dog sired by Major and out of Venus.

A lovely bitch, Babette, sired by Merlin, made her debut in New York

Ch. Santana Mandeville Egghead.
Glamorous stud, used as one of the foundation
sires for the Slippery Hill Basset Kennels.

Ch. Orangepark Dexter.
This was a very popular stud dog in 1970. He
was linebred from Santana-Mandeville stock.

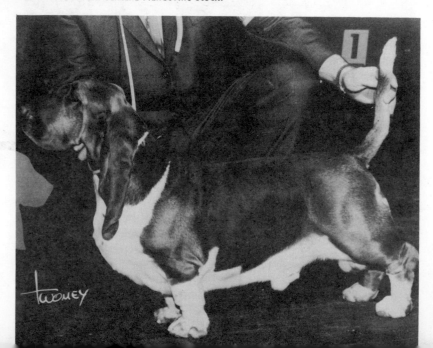

in 1889, shown by Charles Porter of Philadelphia, and Chasseur, by Farmer, was shown by Cornelius Stevenson in New York in 1890.

It might be interesting to note the winnings of the imported dog Nemours, who became a champion of record in America and was the first show type dog of the breed to be imported. He was owned by Maizeland Kennels and his sire was Champion Jupiter (12152—English), out of Vivian (13340—English). Whelped March 21, 1883, bred by Mr. George R. Krehl, Hanover Square, London, his winnings were; first, New York; first, Philadelphia; first, National Breeders' Show, 1884; first and two specials, New Haven; first, Boston; first, New York, 1885; second New York; champion, Boston; first, New York, 1888.

From the above it is easily recognizable that classes at dog shows were, to say the least, slightly different than they are today.

In 1935, at the Detroit dog show, a group of Michigan breeders and fanciers met and formed the Basset Hound Club of America. A dozen prominent breeders were invited, by those present, to become charter members. Careful handling and nurturing of interest in the breed by this enthusiastic group led to wider acceptance of the breed and a slow but sure climb in registrations and recognition of the sterling qualities of the breed.

In 1937 the Basset Hound Club of America qualified as an A.K.C. member club, and in that same year Irish Hills Wallingford, A156785, was the only Basset to complete its bench championship, a considerable feat in the face of a great lack of breed entries at most shows. Mr. and Mrs. Emil Seitz owned and trained Hillcrest Peggy, the first recorded Basset Hound field trial champion in the U.S.

The future of the Basset Hound in America is certainly on a very sound basis. Magnificent animals are being shown in conformation, their quality beyond anything hoped for not too long ago. With these great hounds as a breed basis the Basset cannot help but go on to bigger and better things. The breed has risen from a low eight registrations in 1929 to its present high status in the top ten. Exposure of the public to extremely photogenic specimens on TV, such as Mr. Morgan and Cleo, has certainly helped to further the cause of the breed. Top wins at important shows have also given a boost to the breed and engaged the attention of the dog fancy in general. But there is nothing as fundamentally precious and valuable to the Basset Hound in terms of publicity and its future as its own very evident worth. Whimsical, quaint, clean, lovable, dependable and useful, the Basset has so many plus factors in its favor that its future in the hierarchy of dogs cannot be doubted.

Ch. Santana Mandeville's Sweet Pea
by Ch. Santana Count Dracula x Pretty Penelope
of Mandeville, owned by Mr. and Mrs. Paul E.
Nelson (Santana-Mandeville Basset Kennels).

CHAPTER III

Method of Inheritance

The study and application of genetics to breeding should be particularly interesting to Basset Hound breeders because, though Gregor Mendel is considered the "father" of genetics, a man named Francis Galton, an Englishman, made parallel studies at the same time as Mendel did his work, and Galton used Basset Hounds as a vehicle for his research on coat color inheritance in hounds.

Down through the ages, from the time that early man first became aware of himself as an entity and probed questioningly at the world around him, men of splendid and inquiring minds bent their efforts to shed light upon the mystery of species origin. It remained for one man to find the key to the origin of species; that man was, of course, Charles Robert Darwin. He found the answer to the puzzle of life in evolution, the theory that all life-forms find kinship through a common and basic ancestry and that divergence occurs to permit variety to fit possible changes in environment.

Due to Darwin's principles, science knew that natural selection produced changes in all living things. But how? There seemed to be no rules that could be followed to an end result. There had to be a pattern of inheritance, but what was it and how did it work?

Darwin had asked these questions too, as did the men of science who came after him. But he, like them, could find no definite answer. Darwin did not know that his basic laws of evolution and the fundamental rules of heredity were being developed at approximately the same time. But Darwin's great book, *The Origin of Species,* in which his evolutionary (and revolutionary) theory was advanced, was published in 1859. It was not until 1900, however, that the laws governing inheritable linkage were made known to the world.

In the interim, superstition, arrogant and baseless theorizing, took the place of truth in advancing so-called formulas of inheritance. The inheritance of acquired characteristics is one of the fallacious theories that was widely believed and has its disciples even today. Birthmarking is another false theory which must be discarded in the light of present-day genetical knowledge. The genes which give our dogs all their inheritable material are isolated in the body from any environmental influence. What the host does or has done to him influences them not at all. The so-called "proofs"

Slippery Hill Joyride and Slippery Hill Tamale, snapshots of mother (Tamale) and daughter (Joyride), both taken at three months of age. Here is photographic evidence of how correct head type can be genetically transmitted from one generation to the next.

advanced by the adherents of both these bogus theories were simply isolated coincidences.

Telegony is another of the untrue beliefs about influencing inherited characteristics. This is the theory that the sire of one litter could or would influence the progeny of a future litter out of the same bitch but sired by an entirely different stud. Telegony is, in its essence, comparable to the theory of saturation—which is the belief that if a bitch is bred many times in succession to the same stud, she will become so "saturated" with his "blood" that she will produce only puppies of his type, even when mated to an entirely different stud. By far the strongest and most widely believed was the theory that the blood was the vehicle through which all inheritable material was passed from parents to offspring, from one generation to the next. The taint of that superstition still persists in the phraseology we employ in our breeding terms such as "blood-lines," "percentage of blood," "pure-blooded," "blue-blooded," etc. This "blood" reference in regard to heredity crops up in all places and for all allied references, as witness the politician who cries vehemently, "I am proud that the blood of Paul Revere runs in my veins!" To achieve such a remarkable accomplishment would require transfusion from a long-dead corpse.

THE DISCOVERY OF GENETICS

The truth was found in spite of such a persistent theory, and in the history of science there is no more dramatic story than that of the discovery of the true method of inheritance. No, the truth was not arrived at in some fine endowed scientific laboratory gleaming with the mysterious implements of research. The scene was instead a small dirt garden in Moravia, which is now a part of Czechoslovakia. Here Johann Gregor Mendel, a Moravian monk, planted and crossed several varieties of common garden peas and quietly recorded the differences that occurred through several generations. Over a period of eight years this remarkable man continued his studies. Then, in 1865, he read a paper he had prepared regarding his experiments to the local Brunn, a society of historians and naturalists. The society subsequently published this paper in its journal, which was obscure and definitely limited in distribution.

Now we come to the amazing part of this story, for Mendel's theory of inheritance, which contained the fundamental laws upon which all modern advances in genetics have been based, gathered dust for thirty-four years, and it seemed that one of the most important scientific discoveries of the nineteenth century was to be lost to mankind. Then in 1900, sixteen years after Mendel's death, the paper was rediscovered and his great work given to the world.

In his experiments with the breeding of garden peas, Mendel discovered and identified the units of heredity. He found that when two individual plants which differed in a unit trait were mated, one trait appeared in the offspring, and one did not. The trait which was visible he named the "dominant" trait, and the one which was not visible he called the "recessive" trait. He proposed that traits, such as color, are transmitted by means of units in the sex cells and that one of these units must be pure, let us say either black or white, but never be a mixture of both. From a black parent which is pure for that trait, only black units are transmitted, and from a white parent, only white units can be passed down. But when one parent is black and one is white, a hybrid occurs which transmits both the black and white units in equal amounts. The hybrid itself will take the color

33

of the dominant parent, yet carry the other color as a recessive. Various combinations of unit crosses were tried by Mendel, and he found that there were six possible ways in which a pair of determiners (Mendel's "units") could combine with a similar pair. The Mendelian chart shows how this law of Mendel's operates and the expected results. This simple Mendelian law holds true in the actual breeding of all living things—of plants, mice, humans, or Basset Hounds.

HOW HEREDITY WORKS

The beginning of new life in animals arises from the union of a male sperm and a female egg cell during the process of breeding. Each sperm cell has a nucleus containing one set of chromosomes, which are small packages, or units, of inheritable material. Each egg also possesses a nucleus of one set of chromosomes. The new life formed by the union of sperm cell and egg cell then possesses two sets of chromosomes—one from the sperm, one from the egg, or one set from the sire and one set from the dam. For when the sperm cell enters the egg, it does two things—it starts the egg developing and it adds a set of chromosomes to the set already in the egg. Here is the secret of heredity. For in the chromo-

MENDELIAN EXPECTATION CHART
The six possible ways in which a pair of determinators can unite. Exact expectancy is realized only in numbers 1, 2, and 6.

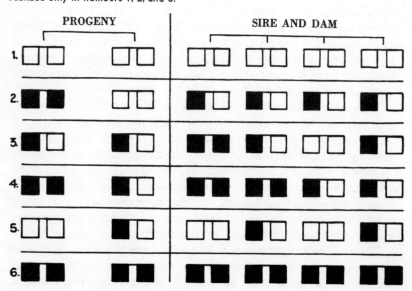

somes lie the living genes that shape the destiny of the unborn young. Thus we see that the pattern of heredity, physical and mental, is transmitted to our dog from its sire and dam through tiny living cells called genes, which are the connecting links between the puppy and his ancestors.

These packets of genes, the chromosomes, resemble long, paired strings of beads. Each pair is alike, the partners formed the same, yet differing from the like partners of the next pair. In the male we find the exception to this rule, for here there is one pair of chromosomes composed of two that are not alike. These are the sex chromosomes, and in the male they are different from those in the female in that the female possesses a like pair while the male does not. If we designate the female chromosomes as X, then the female pair is XX. The male too has an X chromosome, but its partner is a Y chromosome. If the male X chromosome unites with the female X chromosome, then the resulting embryo will be a female. But if the male Y chromosome is carried by the particular sperm that fertilizes the female egg, the resulting progeny will be a male. It is, therefore, a matter of chance as to what sex the offspring will be, since the sperm is capricious and fertilization is random.

The actual embryonic growth of the puppy is a process of division of cells to form more and more new cells and at each cell division of the fertilized egg each of the two sets of chromosomes provided by sire and dam also divide, until all the myriad divisions of cells and chromosomes have reached an amount necessary to form a complete and living entity. Then birth becomes an accomplished fact, and we see before us a living, squealing puppy.

What is he like, this puppy? He is what his controlling genes have made him. His sire and dam have contributed one gene of each kind to their puppy, and this gene which they have given him is but one of the two which each parent possesses for a particular characteristic. Since he has drawn these determiners at random they can be either dominant or recessive genes. His dominant heritage we can see when he develops, but what he possesses in recessive traits is hidden.

There are rules governing dominant and recessive traits useful in summarizing what is known of the subject at the present time. We can be reasonably sure that a dominant trait: (1) Does not skip a generation. (2) Will affect a relatively large number of the progeny. (3) Will be carried only by the affected individuals. (4) Will minimize the danger of continuing undesirable characteristics in a strain. (5) Will make the breeding formula of each individual quite certain.

With recessive traits we note that: (1) The trait may skip one or more generations. (2) On the average a relatively small percentage of the individuals in the strain carry the trait. (3) Only those individuals which

Ch. (Am. and Mex.) Santana-Mandeville Sweet
Pea. Best of Breed, 2nd. in Group, Sun Maid K.C.,
1959. Breeders, owners, handlers, Mr. and Mrs.
Paul E. Nelson, Santana-Mandeville Bassets,
Calif.

carry a pair of determiners for the trait exhibit it. (4) Individuals carrying only one determiner can be ascertained only by mating. (5) The trait must come through both sire and dam.

You will hear some breeders say that the bitch contributes 60 per cent or more to the excellence of the puppies. Others swear that the influence of the sire is greater than that of the dam. Actually, the puppy receives 50 per cent of his germ plasm from each, though one parent may be so dominant that it seems that the puppy received most of his inheritable material from that parent. From the fact that the puppy's parents also both received but one set of determiners from each of their parents and in turn have passed on but one of their sets to the puppy, it would seem that one of those sets that the grandparents contributed has been lost and that therefore the puppy has inherited the germ plasm from only two of its grandparents, not four. But selection is random, and it is possible for the puppy's four grandparents to contribute an equal 25 per cent of all the genes inherited, or various and individual percentages, one grandparent contributing more and another less. It is even possible for the pup to inherit no genes at all from one grandparent and 50 per cent from another.

The genes that have fashioned this puppy of ours are of chemical composition and are living cells securely isolated from any outside influence, a point which we have made before and which bears repeating. Only certain kinds of man-directed radiation, some poisons or other unnatural means can cause change in the genes. No natural means can influence them. Environment can affect an individual but not his germ plasm. For instance, if the puppy's nutritional needs are not fully provided for during his period of growth, his end potential will not be attained; but regardless of his outward appearance, his germ plasm remains inviolate and capable of passing on to the next generation the potential that was denied him by improper feeding.

Breeding fine Bassets would be a simple procedure if all characteristics were governed by simple Mendelian factors, but alas, this is not so. Single genes are not solely responsible for single characteristics, mental or physical. The complexity of any part of the body and its dependence upon other parts in order to function properly make it obvious that we must deal with interlocking blocks of controlling genes in a life pattern of chain reaction. Eye color, for instance, is determined by a simple genetic factor, but the ability to see, the complicated mechanism of the eye, the nerves, the blood supply, the retina and iris, even how your Basset reacts to what he sees, are all part of the genetic pattern of which eye color is but a segment.

Since they are living cells in themselves, the genes can and do change, or mutate. In fact, it is thought now that many more gene mutations take

Ch. Santana-Mandeville Olivia.
Top winning bitch of the famous California
bloodlines. This gorgeous bitch is believed by
many breeders and fanciers to be the ideal
representative of the breed, the standard in
living flesh. Santana-Mandeville Bassets, Mr. and
Mrs. E. Nelson.

Three generations of quality, Fairfield Basset Hounds.

place than were formerly suspected, but that the great majority are either within the animal, where they cannot be seen, or are so small in general scope that they are overlooked. The dramatic mutations which affect the surface are the ones we notice and select for or against according to whether they direct us toward our goal or away from it. Again, with the vagary inherent in all living things, the mutated gene can change once again back to its original form.

We see then that the puppy is the product of his germ plasm, which has been handed down from generation to generation. We know that there are certain rules that generally govern the pattern that the genes form and that a gene which prevents another gene from showing in an individual is said to be a dominant and the repressed gene a recessive. Remember, the animal itself is not dominant or recessive in color or any other characteristic. It is the gene that is dominant or recessive, as judged by results. We find that an animal can contain in each of his body cells a dominant and a recessive gene. When this occurs, the dog is said to be heterozygous. As illustrated in the chart we know that there is an opposite to the heterozygous individual, an animal which contains two genes of the same kind in its cells—either two dominants or two recessives—and this animal is said to be homozygous. The loss of a gene or the gain of a gene, or the process of change among the genes, is known as mutation, and the animal affected is called a mutant.

Every bitch that stands before us, every stud we intend to use, is not just one dog, but two. Every living thing is a Jekyll and Hyde, shadow and substance. The substance is the Basset that lives and breathes and moves before us, the animal that we see, the physical manifestation of the interaction of genotypic characters and environment—the "phenotype." The shadow is the Basset we don't see, yet this shadow is as much a part of the dog before us as the animal we see. This shadow-Basset is the gene-complex, or total collection of its genes—the "genotype." The visual substance is easily evaluated, but the invisible shadow must also be clearly seen and evaluated, for both shadow and substance equally contribute to the generations to come. Without understanding the complete genetic picture of any particular dog, we cannot hope to successfully use that dog to accomplish specific results. In order to understand, we must delve into the genetic background of the animal's ancestry until the shadow becomes as clearly discernible as the substance and we can evaluate the dog's genetic worth as a whole; for this dog that stands before us is but the containing vessel, the custodian of a specific pattern of heredity.

MODERN GENETIC DISCOVERIES

With the basic concept of heredity that Mendel found as a foundation other scientists went forward to fantastic new discoveries in this new and fertile scientific field. The units of inheritance, the genes, were studied and their behavior catalogued. Finally it was found that there was a chemical powder, DNA (deoxyribonucleic acid), and another, similar nucleic acid called RNA (ribonucleic acid) in chromosomes that were, with protein, the materials of heredity.

DNA has complete domination over all cells and is able to constantly reproduce itself. So indescribably minute that it requires an enormous electronic microscope to become visible, it is yet so omniscient that it contains within itself a creative diversity to command uncountable billions of forms. This remarkable chemical is composed of four nucleotides which produce twenty universal amino acids which, in turn, produce over 100,000 proteins that give shape, form and substance to the infinite diversity of life-forms on this earth.

The study of genetics continues as men delve deeper into cause and effect. What we know today of inheritance is of immeasurable importance in animal breeding, removing a great deal of the guesswork from our operations. Yet we do not know enough to make the breeding of top stock a cut-and-dried matter, or to reduce it to the realm of pure science, with a definite answer to every problem. Perhaps this is where the fascination lies. Life is spontaneous and many times unstable, so that even with the greater knowledge that the future will no doubt bring, it is possible that the breeding of top animals will still remain a combination of science and art, with a touch of necessary genius and aesthetic innovation, to ever lend fascination to this riddle of inheritance.

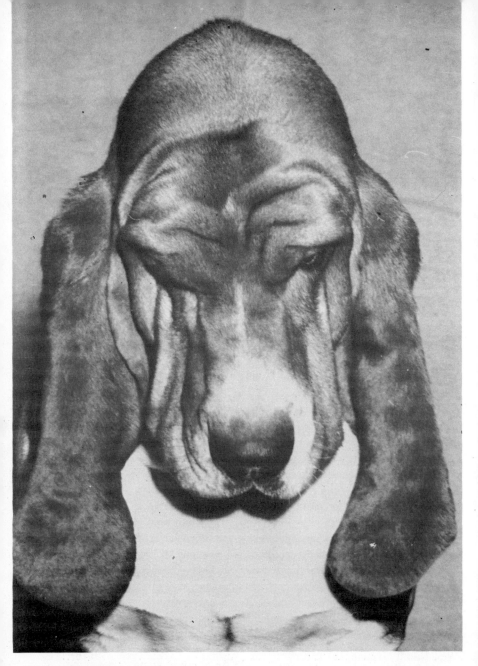

Ch. Santana-Mandeville No-Count.
Photo taken in 1963. Typical of the identifying
wrinkles that form in heavy folds over the head
and face of a quality Basset when his head is
lowered.

CHAPTER IV

Basic Breeding Techniques

In today's mechanistic world, with its rushing pace and easy pleasures, much of the creative urge in man has been throttled. We who breed dogs are extremely fortunate, for in our work we have a real creative outlet—we are in the position of being able to mold beauty and utility in living flesh and blood. Our tools are the genes of inheritance, and our art, their infinite combination. We have the power to create a work of living art that will show the evidence of our touch for generations to come.

Now that we have absorbed some of the basic facts of heredity, we can, with greater understanding, examine the various kinds of breeding which can be used in perpetuating wanted characteristics. We have learned that within the design of the germ plasm great variation occurs. But within the breed itself as a whole, we have an average, or norm, which the great majority of Bassets mirror. Draw a straight horizontal line on a piece of paper and label this line, "norm." Above this line draw another and label it, "above norm." This latter line represents the top dogs, the great ones, and the length of this line will be very much shorter than the length of the "norm" line. Below the "norm" line draw still another line, designating this to be, "below norm." These are the animals possessing faults which we do not wish to perpetuate.

Since the time of the first registered Bassets the number of breeders who have molded the characteristics of the breed have been legion. So many have bred without a basic knowledge of any of the fundamentals that the stock produced has the detrimental effect of dangerously lowering the norm. Examine the pedigrees of your dogs, and in many instances you will find an example of this—a line incorporated in your pedigree that causes worry to the true student of breeding. The real objective of all breeding is to raise the norm of a given breed and thereby approach always closer to the breed standard.

If we are to achieve the greatest good from any program of breeding,

For more comprehensive information on the art of breeding, see the author's book DOG BREEDERS' HANDBOOK.

there are four important traits which we must examine. It is essential that these traits should never depart from the norm.

The first is fertility. The lack of this essential in any degree must be guarded against diligently.

The second is vigor. Loss of vigor, or hardiness, and its allied ills, such as lowered resistance to disease, finicky eating, etc., will lead to disaster.

Longevity is the third important trait. An individual of great worth— who represents a fortunate combination of excellent characteristics which he dominantly passes on to his offspring—must be useful for a long time after his or her worth is recognized by the progeny produced.

The fourth is temperament. Here is the sum total of the dog's usefulness to man in the various categories in which he serves. Lack of true Basset character nullifies any other advances which you may make in your breeding program.

The norm can be likened to the force of gravity, possessing a powerful pull toward itself, so that regression toward the average is strong, even though you have used in your breeding parents which are both above average. The same holds true for progeny bred from animals below norm, but from these you will get a lesser number which reach the mean average and a greater number which remain below norm. In the case of the better-than-average parents, some of the progeny will stay above the norm line and the majority will regress. Occasionally a dog of superior structure is produced by a poor family, but inevitably this animal is useless as a stud because he will produce all his objectionable family traits and none of the fortuitous characteristics he displays in himself. From a breeding stand-point it is far better to use an average individual from top stock than a top individual from average or below-average stock. It is also true that many times a great show dog produces average progeny while his little-known brother, obscured by the shadow of the great dog's eminence, produces many above-average young. This is not as strange as it sounds when we consider the fact that the individual animal is the custodian of his germ plasm and it is this germ plasm that produces, not the individual. In this instance, due to variation in the germ plasm, the top dog does not possess the happy genetic combinations that his average brother does and so cannot produce stock of comparative value.

Any of the various categories of breeding practice which we will outline can be followed for the betterment of the breed if used intelligently. Regardless of which practice one follows, there generally comes a time when it is necessary to incorporate one or more of the other forms into the breeding program in order to concentrate certain genetic characters, or to introduce new ones which are imperative for over-all balance. Out-cross breeding is not recommended as a consistent practice. Rather, it is

a valuable adjunct to the other methods when used as a corrective measure.

INBREEDING

By breeding father to daughter, half brother to half sister, son to mother, and, by closest inbreeding of all, brother to sister, stability and purity of inherited material is obtained. Specifically, inbreeding concentrates both good features and faults, strengthening dominants and bringing recessives out into the open where they can be seen and evaluated. It supplies the breeder with the only control he can have over prepotency and homozygosity, or the combining and balancing of similar genetic factors. Inbreeding does not produce degeneration, it merely concentrates weaknesses already present so that they can be recognized and eliminated. This applies to both physical and psychical hereditary transmission.

The most important phases of inbreeding are: (1) To choose as nearly faultless partners as is possible; (2) To cull, or select, rigidly from the resultant progeny.

Selection is always important regardless of which breeding procedure is used, but in inbreeding it becomes imperative. It is of interest to note that the most successful inbreeding programs have used as a base an animal which was either inbred or line-bred. To the breeder, the inbred animal represents an individual whose breeding formula has been so simplified that certain results can almost always be depended upon.

There are many examples of extreme inbreeding over a period of generations in other animal and plant life. Perhaps the most widely known are the experimental rats bred by Dr. Helen L. King, which are the result of over one hundred generations of direct brother and sister mating. The end result has been bigger, finer rodents than the original pair, and entirely dependable uniformity. Dr. Leon F. Whitney has bred and developed a beautiful strain of tropical fish, *Lebistes reticulatis*, commonly known as "guppies," by consecutive brother to sister breeding for ten generations. Dr. Whitney found that each succeeding generation was a little smaller and less vigorous, but that in the fifth generation a change occurred for the better, and in each generation thereafter, size, vigor, and color improved. This pattern should hold true with all life forms developed from the same type of breeding.

It is interesting to note that genetic experiments with plants, vegetables, and animals which we consider lower in the evolutionary scale than our beloved dogs have shown that when two intensely inbred lines of consecutive brother and sister matings are crossed, the resultant progeny are larger than the original heterozygous stock and possess hybrid vigor such as the mongrel possesses, which enables him to exist even under environmental neglect; the technical term for hybrid vigor is heterosis.

Can dog breeders indulge in such concentrated inbreeding with stock as has been attempted successfully by scientists with other genetic material? We don't know, simply because, to our knowledge, it has never been tried. It would be an expensive undertaking to keep two or more lines progressing of direct brother and sister inbreedings; to cull and destroy, always keeping the best pair as breeding partners for the next generation. Lethal faults, hitherto unsuspected in the stock, might become so drastically concentrated as to bring the experiment to a premature conclusion, even if one had the time, money, and energy to attempt it. But such is the inherent character of germ plasm that one direct outcross will bring complete normality to an inbred line drastically weakened by its own concentrated faults.

It is essential that the breeder have a complete understanding of the merits of inbreeding, for by employing it skillfully results can be obtained to equal those found in other animal-breeding fields. We must remember that inbreeding in itself creates neither faults nor virtues, it merely strengthens and fixes them in the resulting animals. If the basic stock used is generally good, possessing but few, and those minor, faults, then inbreeding will concentrate all those virtues which are so valuable in that basic stock. Inbreeding gives us great breeding worth by its unique ability to produce prepotency and unusual similarity of type. It exposes the "skeletons in the closet" by bringing to light hitherto hidden faults, so that they may be selected against. We do not correct faults by inbreeding, therefore, we merely make them recognizable so they can be eliminated. The end result of inbreeding, coupled with rigid selection, is complete stability of the breeding material.

With certain strains inbreeding can be capricious, revealing organic weaknesses never suspected that result in decreased vitality, abnormalities—physical and mental—or lethal or crippling factors. Unfortunately, it is not possible to foretell results when embarking on such a program, even if seemingly robust and healthy breeding partners are used as a base. The best chance of success generally comes from the employment of animals which themselves have been strongly inbred and have not been appreciably weakened by it in any way.

An interesting development frequently found in inbreeding is in the extremes produced. The average progeny from inbreeding is equal to the average from line-breeding or outbreeding, but the extremes are greater than those produced by either of the latter breeding methods. Inbreeding, then, is at once capable of producing the best and the worst, and these degrees can be found present in the same litter.

Here again, in inbreeding, as in most of the elements of animal husbandry, we must avoid thinking in terms of human equations. Whether for good or ill, your Basset was man-made, and his destiny and that of his progeny lie in your hands. By selection you improve the strain, culling and killing misfits and monsters. Mankind indulges in no such practice of purification of the race. He mates without any great mental calculation or plan for the future generation. His choice of a mate is both geographically and socially limited in scope. No one plans this mating of his for the future betterment of the breed. Instead, he is blindly led by emotions labeled "love," and sometimes by lesser romantics, "desire." For our Basset we want something vastly better than the hit-and-miss proposition that has been the racial procedure of man.

Another type of inbreeding, which is not practiced as much as it should be, is "backcrossing." Here we think largely in terms of the male dog, since the element of time is involved. The process involves finding a superior breeding male who is so magnificent in type that we want to perpetuate his qualities and produce, as closely as we can, the prototype of this certain individual. This good male is bred to a fine bitch, and the best female pup who is similar to her sire in type is bred back again to her sire. Again, the best female pup is selected and bred back to her sire. This is continued as long as the male can reproduce, or until weaknesses become apparent (if they do) that make it impractical to continue. If this

Cinnamon

Paprika

Nutmeg

Linebreeding produces consistency of type and genetic control. Here are three sisters, Slippery Hill Cinnamon, Ch. Slippery Hill Paprika, and Ch. Slippery Hill Nutmeg. Note the complete similarity in type and quality. The sisters are from Dr. Skolnick's Slippery Hill Kennels.

excellent male seems to have acquired his superiority through the genetic influence of his mother, the first breeding made should possibly be the mating of son to mother, and the subsequent breeding as described above. In each litter the bitch retained to backcross to her sire should, of course, greatly mirror the sire's type.

LINE-BREEDING

Line-breeding is a broader kind of inbreeding that conserves valuable characteristics by concentration and in a general sense gives us some control of type but a lesser control over specific characteristics. It creates "strains," or "families," within the breed which are easily recognized by their similar conformation. This is the breeding method used by most of the larger kennels, with varied success, since it is not extreme and therefore relatively safe. It is also the method the neophyte is generally advised to employ, for the same reasons.

Specifically, line-breeding entails the selection of breeding partners who have, in their pedigrees, one or more common ancestors. These individuals (or individual) occur repeatedly within the first four or five generations, so that it can be assumed their genetic influence molds the type of succeeding generations. It is a fact that in many breeds success has been obtained by line-breeding to outstanding individuals.

The method varies greatly in intensity, so that some dogs may be strongly line-bred, while others only remotely so. Selection is an important factor here, too, for if we line-breed to procure the specific type of a certain fine animal, then we must select in succeeding generations breeding stock which is the prototype of that individual, or our reason for line-breeding is lost.

One of the chief dangers of line-breeding can be contributed by the breeder of the strain. Many times the breeder reaches a point where he selects his breeding partners on pedigree alone, instead of by individual selection and pedigree combined, within the line.

In some instances intense line-breeding, particularly when the individual line-bred is known to be prepotent, can have all the strength of direct inbreeding.

To found a strain which has definite characteristics, within the breed, the following recommendations, based mainly on the work of Humphrey and Warner, and Kelley and Whitney, can be used as a guide.

1. Decide what few traits are essential and what faults are intolerable. Vigor, fertility, character, and temperament must be included in these essentials.

2. Develop a scoring system and score selected virtues and faults in accordance with your breeding aim. Particular stress should be put upon scoring for individual traits which need improvement.

3. Line-breed consistently to the best individuals produced which, by the progeny test, show that they will further improve the strain. Inbreeding can be indulged in if the animal used is of exceptional quality and with no outstanding faults. Outcrossings can be made to bring in wanted characteristics if they are missing from the basic stock. Relationship need not be close in the foundation animals, since wide outcrosses will give greater variation and therefore offer a much wider selection of desirable trait combinations.

Every Basset used in this breeding program to establish a strain must be rigidly assessed for individual and breeding excellence and the average excellence of its relatives and its progeny.

OUTCROSS BREEDING

Outcross breeding is the choosing of breeding partners whose pedigrees, in the first five or six generations, are free from any common ancestry. With our Bassets we cannot outcross in the true sense of the term, since the genetic basis of all Bassets is built upon the germ plasm of a few selected individuals. To outcross completely, using the term literally (complete heterozygosity), it would be necessary to use an individual of an alien breed as one of the breeding partners.

For the breeder to exercise any control over the progeny of an outcross mating, one of the partners should be inbred or closely line-bred. The other partner should show, in himself and by the progeny test when bred to other bitches, that he is dominant in the needed compensations which are the reasons for the outcross. Thus, by outcross breeding, we bring new and needed characteristics into a strain, along with greater vigor and, generally, a lack of uniformity in the young. Greater uniformity can be achieved if the outcross is made between animals of similar family type. Here again we have a breeding method which has produced excellent individuals, since it tends to conceal recessive genes and promote individual merit. But it generally leads to a lower breeding worth in the outbred animal by dispersing favorable genetic combinations which have given us strain uniformity.

Outcross breeding can be likened to a jigsaw puzzle. We have a puzzle made up of pieces of various shapes and sizes which when fitted together form a certain pattern. This basic puzzle is comparable to our line-bred or inbred strain. But in this puzzle there are a few pieces that we would like to change, and in so doing change the finished puzzle pattern for the better. We outcross by removing some of the pieces and reshaping them to our fancy, remembering that these new shapes also affect the shapes of the adjoining pieces, which must then be slightly altered for perfect fit. When this has been successfully accomplished, the finished pattern has been altered to suit our pleasure—we hope.

It sometimes happens that a line-bred or inbred bitch will be outcross bred to a stud possessed of an open pedigree. It would be assumed by the breeder that the bitch's family type would dominate in the resulting progeny. But occasionally the stud proves himself to be strongly pre-potent, and the young instead reflect his individual qualities, not those of the bitch. This can be good or bad, depending on what you are looking for in the resultant litter.

Incidentally, when we speak of corrective, or compensation, breeding, we do not mean the breeding of extremes to achieve an intermediate effect. Corrective, or compensation, breeding means the breeding of one partner which is lacking, or faulty, in any specific respect to an animal which is normal or excellent in the particular area where the other partner is found lacking. In the resulting progeny we can expect to find some young which show the desired improvement.

To sum up briefly, we find that *inbreeding* brings us a fixity of type and simplifies the breeding formula. It strengthens desirable dominants and brings hidden and undesirable recessives to the surface where they can be recognized and possibly corrected by *outcross breeding*. When we have thus established definite improvement in type by rigid selection for wanted characteristics, we *line-breed* to create and establish a strain or family line which, in various degrees, incorporates and produces the improvements which have been attained.

In this maze of hidden and obvious genetic stirring, we must not forget the importance of the concrete essence that stands before us. The breeding partners must be examined as individuals in themselves, apart from the story their pedigrees tell us. For as individuals they have been fashioned by, and are the custodians of, their germ plasm, and mirror this fact in their being. Breedings made from paper study only are akin to human marriages arranged in youth by a third party without consulting the partners—they can be consummated but have small chance of success.

The importance of a pedigree lies in the knowledge we have of the individual animals involved. A fifteen-generation pedigree means nothing if we know nothing about the dogs mentioned. It is more important to extend your knowledge of three or four generations than to extend the pedigree itself. Of real guidance in breeding is a card-index system. This system should indicate clearly the faults and virtues of every pedigree name for at least three generations, with available information as to dominant and recessive traits and the quality of each animal's progeny. At the moment, such a system is practically impossible to achieve. There is little enough known, genetically, about living animals, and the virtues of dogs that are gone are distorted by time and sentiment.

The breeding of fine dogs is not a toy to be played with by children. For some of us it forms a nucleus of living, in the esthetic sense. We who give much of our time, thought, and energy to the production of superior stock are often disgusted and disillusioned by the breeding results of others who merely play at breeding. So often individuals long in the game advise the novice never to inbreed, but only to line-breed, since in this way the least harm can be done. There has been too much harm done already by novice breeders who should not have been encouraged to breed at all, except under the direct supervision or advice of an experienced or knowledgeable dog man.

The people who compose what we term the Basset Hound "fancy" belong to one of three categories: the novice, the amateur, and the professional. The novice is one who has recently become enamored of the breed, a tyro, a beginner. Many of them remain in that category indefinitely, due to lack of sincerity or reluctance to learn. Others, eager to absorb all they can, soon rise above the original status.

The professional is one who makes his livelihood from the dog game. His living or employment depends in whole or part upon his kennel and field training activities. A professional must know his business well in order to make it a success, and the earnest professional generally does.

Numerically, the largest category is that of the amateur. To these individuals the breeding, showing, hunting or training of Bassets is a serious hobby. Here are the students of the breed, the people who, in most instances, are well informed, yet avid for new knowledge that will aid in breed betterment.

Our novice is many times a charming person who loves his dogs passionately, provides them with more fancy vitamins and supplements than honest food, and treats them with a sloppy sentimentality that even a human baby would resent. He simply can't wait to breed his lovely bitch and have those adorable puppies. Of course he hasn't the time to acquire a bit of knowledge about the breed, or about the animals in his bitch's pedigree or the stud to which he is going to breed. How then will he have the time or knowledge to care for the pregnant bitch and the subsequent litter properly? Yet inevitably he does find time to listen to the pseudo-professional advice of several self-confessed authorities. In due time this novice is possessed of a litter of the cutest puppies you ever saw, which will in turn be sold to other novices (Heaven help them) as show and breeding prospects.

By far the greatest menace to the future of the breed is a particular type of wealthy novice. Possessed of the wherewithal to keep and breed any amount of dogs, trainers to train them, and kennelmen to take care of them, this novice blunders arrogantly forward by virtue of the authority vested in him by his bankbooks and, unhampered by knowledge, breeds indiscriminately, producing litter upon litter of worthless stock. By the law of averages an occasional animal is produced that is fairly good. In the end this novice generally, surprisingly and suddenly, blossoms out as a full blown "authority" and judge.

What has been written above is not to be construed as a sweeping condemnation of all novices. Without a constant influx of neophyte breeders, the breed would not be in the high place it is today. Many so-called novices bring to their new breed interest a vast store of canine knowledge collected by an inquiring mind and contact with other breeds.

To repeat, the novice is generally advised by the old-time breeder to begin his new hobby with a line-bred bitch, as this is the cautious approach which leaves the least margin for error. But what of that novice who is essentially what we call a born "dog man"? That individual who, for lack of better definition, we say has a "feel" for dogs, who seems to possess an added sense where dogs are concerned?

If this person has an inquiring mind, normal intelligence, and has been associated with other breeds, then the picture of him as the true novice changes. The old-timer will find many times that this "novice" frequently possesses information that the old-timer did not even know existed. This is especially true if the tyro has been exposed to some scientific learning in fields relative to animal advancement. Even experience, which is the old-timer's last-ditch stand, is negligible, for this knowledgeable "novice" can disregard the vagaries of experience with foreknowledge of expectancy.

In most instances this type of novice doesn't begin to think of breeding, or even owning a specimen of the breed, until he has made a thorough study of background, faults, virtues, and genetic characters. To him, imitation is not a prelude to success. Therefore the line-bred bitch, modeled by another's ego, is not for him. The outcross bitch, whose genetic composition presents a challenge and which, by diligent study and application of acquired knowledge, can become the fountainhead of a strain of his own, is the answer to his need.

Some of what you have read here in reference to the novice may have seemed to be cruel caricature. Actually, it is not caricature, but it is cruel and is meant to stress a point. We realize that to some novices our deep absorption in all the many aspects of breed betterment may seem silly or ridiculous. But the genetic repercussion of breeding stupidity can echo down through generations, making a mockery of our own intense, sometimes heartbreaking, and often humble, striving toward an ideal.

Ch. Santana Count Dracula by Belbay Chevalier
x Ch. Beautiful Minnetonkie, Santana-Mandeville
Basset Kennels.

CHAPTER V

Feeding

Your Basset is a carnivore, a flesh eater. His teeth are not made for grinding as are human teeth, but are chiefly fashioned for tearing and severing. Over a period of years this fact has led to the erroneous conclusion that the dog must be fed mostly on muscle meat in order to prosper. Wolves, jackals, wild dogs, and foxes comprise the family Canidae to which your dog belongs. These wild relatives of the dog stalk and run down their living food in the same manner the dog would employ if he had not become attached to man. The main prey of these predators are the various hoofed herbivorous animals, small mammals and birds of their native habitat. The carnivores consume the entire body of their prey, not just the muscle meat alone. This manner of feeding has led some zoologists to consider the dog family as omnivorous (eater of both plant and animal matter), despite their obvious physical relationship to the carnivores.

You would assume, and rightly so, that the diet which keeps these wild cousins of the dog strong, healthy, and fertile could be depended upon to do the same for your Basset. Of course, in this day and age your dog cannot live off the land. He depends upon you for sustenance, and to feed him properly you must understand what essential food values the wild carnivore derives from his kill, for this is nature's supreme lesson in nutrition.

The canine hunter first laps the blood of his victim, then tears open the stomach and eats its contents, composed of predigested vegetable matter. He feasts on liver, heart, kidneys, lungs, and the fat-encrusted intestines. He crushes and consumes the bones and the marrow they contain, feeds on fatty meat and connective tissue, and finally eats the lean muscle meat. From the blood, bones, marrow, internal organs, and muscle meat he has absorbed minerals and proteins. The stomach and its contents have supplied vitamins and carbohydrates. From the intestines and fatty meat he gets fats, fatty acids, vitamins, and carbohydrates. Other proteins come from the ligaments and connective tissue. Hair and some indigestible parts of the intestinal contents provide enough roughage for proper laxation. From the sun he basks in and the water he drinks, he absorbs supplementary vitamins and minerals. From his kill, therefore, the carnivore acquires a well-rounded diet. To supply these same essen-

tials to your Basset in a form which you can easily purchase is the answer
to his dietary needs.

BASIC FOODS AND SUPPLEMENTS

From the standpoint of nutrition, any substance may be considered
food which can be used by an animal as a body-building material, a source
of energy, or a regulator of body activity. From the preceding paragraphs
we have learned that muscle meat alone will not fill these needs and that
your Basset's diet must be composed of many other food materials to
provide elements necessary to his growth and health. These necessary
ingredients can be found in any grocery store. There you can buy all the
important natural sources of the dietary essentials listed below.

1. PROTEIN: meat, dairy products, eggs, soybeans.
2. FAT: butter, cream, oils, fatty meat, milk, cream cheese, suet.
3. CARBOHYDRATES: cereals, vegetables, confectionery syrups, honey.
4. VITAMIN A: greens, peas, beans, asparagus, broccoli, eggs, milk.
5. THIAMINE: vegetables, legumes, whole grains, eggs, muscle meats, organ
   meats, milk, yeast.
6. RIBOFLAVIN: green leaves, milk, liver, cottonseed flour or meal, egg yolk,
   wheat germ, yeast, beef, chicken.
7. NIACIN: milk, lean meats, liver, yeast.
8. VITAMIN D: fish that contains oil (salmon, sardine, herring, cod), fish
   liver oils, eggs, fortified milk.
9. ASCORBIC ACID: tomatoes, citrus fruits, raw cabbage (it has not been
   established that ascorbic acid is necessary for dogs).
10. IRON, CALCIUM, AND PHOSPHORUS: milk and milk products, vege-
    tables, eggs, soybeans, bone marrow, blood, liver, oatmeal.

The first three listed essentials complement each other and compose
the basic nutritional needs. Proteins build new body tissue and are composed of amino acids, which differ in combination with the different
proteins. Carbohydrates furnish the fuel for growth and energy, and fat
produces heat which becomes energy and enables the dog to store energy
against emergency. Vitamins and minerals, in general, act as regulators
of cell activity.

Proteins are essentially the basis of life, for living cells are composed of
protein molecules. In this connection, an interesting scientific experiment
was conducted a short while ago which led to an important discovery. A
young scientist attempted to duplicate the conditions which, it is assumed,
prevailed upon the earth before life began. Cosmological theory indicates
that the atmosphere at that time (approximately two thousand million
years ago, give or take a year) would have been poisonous to all the living
organisms that exist today, with the exception of certain bacteria. When

the experiment had been completed, it was found that amino acids had formed. These chemicals are the building blocks of proteins, and proteins are the basis of life. No, science has not yet produced actual life by building proteins. It is still rather difficult to even define life, let alone manufacture it. But we can sustain and give growth to living forms by proper feeding procedures.

The main objective in combining food factors is to mix them in the various amounts necessary to procure a balanced diet. This can be done in a number of ways. The essential difference in the many good methods of feeding lies in the time it takes to prepare the food and in the end cost of the materials used. Dogs can be fed expensively and they can be fed cheaply, and in each instance they can be fed equally well.

There are various food products on the market packaged specifically for canine consumption. The quality of these foods as complete diets in themselves ranges from poor to excellent. The better *canned*, or *pudding*, foods are good but expensive for feeding a number of dogs. Compact and requiring no preparation, the canned foods are fine for use at shows or when traveling—though for traveling an even better diet is biscuits, lean meat, and very little water. The result is less urination and defeca-

Use one or another of the various commercial foods packaged for canine consumption. They are generally carefully made and contain blended food elements.

tion, since the residue from this diet is very small. The diet is, of course, not to be fed over any extended period of time because it lacks food value.

Biscuits can be considered as tidbits rather than food, since much of the vitamin and mineral content has been destroyed by baking. The same holds true for *kibbled* foods. They are fillers to which must be added fat, milk, broths, meat, vegetables, and vitamin and mineral supplement.

By far the most complete of the manufactured foods are the *grain foods*. In such a highly competitive business as the manufacturing and merchandising of these foods, it is essential for the manufacturer to market a highly palatable and balanced ration. The better grain foods have constantly changing formulas to conform to the most recent results of scientific dietary research. They are, in many cases, the direct result of controlled generation tests in scientific kennels where their efficacy can be ascertained. A good grain food should not be considered merely a filler. Rather, it should be employed as the basic diet to which fillers might possibly be added. Since the grain food is bag or box packaged and not hermetically sealed, the fat content is necessarily low. A high degree of fat would produce quick rancidity. Therefore fat must be added to the dry food. Milk, which is one of the finest of foods in itself, can be added along with broths or plain warm water to arrive at the proper consistency for palatability. With such a diet we have a true balance of essentials, wastage is kept to a minimum, stools are small and firm and easily removed, and cost and labor have been reduced to the smallest equation possible to arrive at and yet feed well. The *pellet type* food is simply grain food to which a binding agent has been added to hold the grains together in the desired compact form.

Fat should be introduced into the dog's diet in its pure form. Proteins and carbohydrates are converted into fat by the body. Fat also causes the dog to retain his food longer in the stomach. It stores vitamins E, K, A, and D, and lessens the bulk necessary to be fed at each meal. Fat can be melted and poured over the meal, or put through the meat grinder and then mixed with the basic ration.

Just as selection is important in breeding, so ratio is important in feeding. The proper diet must not only provide all the essentials, it must also supply those essentials in the proper proportions. This is what we mean by a balanced diet. It can be dangerous to your Basset's well being if the ratios of any of his dietary essentials are badly unbalanced over a period of time. The effects can be disastrous in the case of puppies. This is the basic reason for putting your faith in a good, scientifically balanced grain dog food.

There is an abundance of concentrated *vitamin supplements* on the market specifically manufactured for dogs. They are undoubtedly of real worth—if your dog needs a supplement. Dogs fed a balanced diet do not need additional concentrated supplements, with the exception, perhaps, of the rare individual. If you feel that your dog is in need of a supplement, it is wiser to consult your veterinarian for advice and specific dosage. Check the label of the dog food you buy to make sure that it has all the necessary ingredients. If it has, you will not find it necessary to pour in concentrated, highly expensive supplements. Another of the supplements widely in use and packaged under various trade names embodies the elements of what was initially called A.P.F., or animal protein factor. This is a powder combining various antibiotic residues with the composite vitamin B_{12}. The role of this supplement in dog feeding has not, as yet, been adequately established. Theoretically, it is supposed that this supplement produces better food utilization and the production of body fat.

In many instances kennel owners feel that their animals, for various reasons, need a supplementary boost in their diet. Some are in critical stages of growth, bitches are about to be bred or are in whelp, mature dogs are being frequently used for stud, and others are recuperating from illness. In such cases supplements can be added to the food, but in reasonable amounts. It is better, too, to supply the supplements through the medium of natural nutritional material rather than chemical, concentrated, commercial supplements. Brewers' yeast, alfalfa meal, and similar natural agents can be mixed separately in a container and judicious quantities added to the basic diet.

Calcium and *phosphorus* in pure chemical form must be handled with care when used in the dog's diet. Toxic conditions can be caused by an over-abundance of this material in the bloodstream. Green, ground, edible bone meal is a much better product to use where it is thought necessary. Most good grain foods have an abundance of this inexpensive element in correct balance. Milk is a highly desirable vehicle for balanced calcium and phosphorus as well as many other nutritional needs.

Cod liver oil is another product that, if given to excess over a period of time, can cause toxicity and bone malformation. It is better and cheaper to employ a fish liver oil concentrate such as percomorph oil. In this oil the base vehicle has been discarded and the pure oil concentrated, so that a very small dosage is required. Many owners and breeders pour cod liver oil and throw handsful of calcium and supplementary concentrates into the food pans in such lavish amounts that there is a greater bulk of these than of the basic food, on the theory that, if a little does some good, a greater amount will be of immense benefit. This concept is both ridiculous and dangerous.

An occasional pinch of *bicarbonate of soda* in the food helps to neutralize stomach acidity and can prevent, or alleviate, fatigue caused by a highly acid diet. Bones need never be fed to dogs for food value if the diet is complete. Poultry bones should never be fed. They splinter into sharp shards which can injure gums or rip the throat lining or intestines. Once in the stomach they are dissolved by strong gastric juices. It is on their way to their ultimate goal that they do damage. The same is also true of fishbones. Soft rib bones are excellent to feed your dog periodically, not necessarily as nourishment, but to clean his teeth. The animal's teeth pierce through them completely, and in so doing tartar will be removed and the teeth kept clean of residue. These soft rib bones can be considered the canine's toothbrush. Nylon and rawhide manufactured bones serve the same purpose.

Table scraps are always good, and if your dog is a good eater and easy keeper, give him any leftovers in his food pan, including potatoes. The diets of good feeders can be varied to a greater extent without unfavorable repercussions than can the diets of finicky eaters. Fish is a good food, containing all the food elements which are found in meat, with a bonus of extra nutritional values. *Muscle meat* lacks many essentials and is so low in calcium that, even when supplemented with vitamin D, there is grave danger of rickets developing. In its raw state, meat is fre-

NYLABONE is a necessity product available at your local pet shop (not sold in supermarkets). The puppy or grown dog chews the hambone-flavored nylon into a frilly dog toothbrush, massaging his gums and cleaning his teeth as he plays. Veterinarians highly recommend this product . . . but beware of cheap imitations that might splinter or break. The photo shows a new NYLABONE and one that has been chewed.

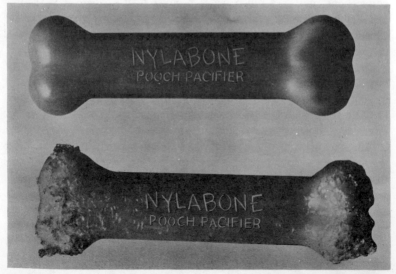

quently the intermediate host of several forms of internal parasites. Meat by-products and canned meat, which generally contains by-products, are much better as food for dogs than pure muscle meat. Incidentally, whale meat, which is over 80 per cent protein, could well replace horse meat, which is less than 50 per cent protein, in the dog's diet.

Water is one of the elementary nutritional essentials. Considering the fact that the dog's body is approximately 70 per cent water, which is distributed in varying percentages throughout the body tissues and organs, including the teeth and bones, it isn't difficult to realize the importance of this staple to the dog's well being. Water flushes the system, stimulates gastric juice activity, brings about better appetite, and acts as a solvent within the body. It is one of the major sources of necessary minerals and helps during hot weather, and to a lesser degree during winter, to regulate the dog's temperature. When a dog is kept from water for any appreciable length of time, dehydration occurs. This is a serious condition, a fact which is known to any dog owner whose animal has been affected by diarrhea, continuous nausea, or any of the diseases in which this form of body shrinkage occurs.

Water is the cheapest part of your dog's diet, so supply it freely, particularly in warm weather. In winter if snow and ice are present and available to your Basset, water is not so essential. At any rate, if left in a bucket in his run, it quickly turns to ice. Yet even under these conditions it is an easy matter to bring your dog in and supply him with at least one good drink of fresh water during the day. Being so easily provided, so inexpensive, and so highly essential to your Basset's health, sober thought dictates that we should allow our dogs to "take to drink."

Breeders with only a few dogs can sometimes afford the extra time, expense, and care necessary to feed a varied and complicated diet. But it is easy to see that to feed a large kennel in such fashion would take an immense amount of time, labor, and expense. Actually, the feeding of a scientifically balanced grain food as the basic diet eliminates the element of chance which exists in diets prepared by the kennel owner from natural sources, since overabundance of some specific elements, as well as a lack of others, can bring about dietary ills and deficiencies.

Caloric requirements vary with age, temperament, changes in temperature, and activity. If your dog is nervous, very active, young, and kept out-of-doors in winter, his caloric intake must be greater than the phlegmatic, underactive, fully grown dog who has his bed in the house. Keep your dog in good flesh, neither too fat nor too thin. You are the best judge of the amount to feed him to keep him in his best condition. A well-fed Basset should always be in show "bloom"—clear-eyed, glossy-coated, filled with vim and vigor, and with enough of an all-over layer of fat.

Use a narrow bowl from which to feed your
Basset. The idea is to allow his ears to fall on
each side of the bowl and so keep from getting
food soaked.

FEEDING TECHNIQUES

The consistency of the food mix can vary according to your Basset's
taste. It is best not to serve the food in too sloppy a mixture, except in
the case of very young puppies. It is also good practice to feed the same
basic ration at every meal so that the taste of the food does not vary
greatly at each feeding. Constant changing of the diet, with supplementary meals of raw or cooked meat, tends to produce finicky eaters,
the bane of the kennel and private owner's existence. Never leave the food
pan before your dog for more than thirty minutes. If he hasn't eaten by
then, or has merely nibbled, the pan should be removed and not presented
to him again until his next feeding time. This same policy should be
followed when breaking a dog to a new diet. If he has become a canine
gourmet, spoiled by a delicate diet, he may sometimes refuse to eat for
two or three days. But eventually, when his hunger becomes acute enough
and he realizes his hunger strike will not result in coddling and the bringing forth of his former delicacies, he will eat with gusto whatever is put

before him. Remember, your Basset is not a lap dog—he is an energetic sporting dog and should not be babied. Where there are several dogs to create mealtime competition, there is little danger of finicky eaters regardless of what is fed.

Keep your feeding utensils clean to eliminate the danger of bacterial formation and sourness, especially in warm weather. Your food pans can be of any solid metal material. Agate, porcelain, and the various types of enamelware have a tendency to chip, and are therefore not desirable.

Every kennel owner and breeder has his own pet diet which has proven successful in the rearing and maintenance of his stock. In each instance he will insist that his is the only worth-while diet, and he cannot be blamed for so asserting, since his particular diet has nourished and kept his own stock in top condition over a period of years. Yet the truth is, as we have mentioned before in this chapter, that there are many ways to feed dogs and feed them well, and no one diet can be said to be the best.

Remember always that feeding ranks next to breeding in the influence it exerts on the growing dog. Knowledgeable breeding can produce genetically fine specimens, selection can improve the strain and the breed, but, without full and proper nourishment, particularly over the period of growth, the dog cannot attain to the promise of his heritage. The brusque slogan of a famous cattle breeder might well be adopted by breeders of Bassets. The motto is, "Breed, feed, weed."

Ch. Santana-Mandeville Rodney, shown winning
Best of Breed at the Potomac Basset Hound
Specialty Show at seven years of age (1967).
Note the truly fabulous male type of this
outstanding dog.

CHAPTER VI

General Care

When you own a dog, you own a dependent. Though the Internal Revenue Department does not recognize this fact, it is nevertheless true. Whatever pleasure one gets out of life must be paid for in some kind of coin, and this is as applicable to the pleasure we derive from our dogs as it is in all things. With our dogs we pay the toll of constant care. This Basset which you have taken into your home and made a part of your family life depends completely upon you for his every need. In return for the care you give him, he repays you with a special brand of love and devotion that can't be duplicated. That is the bargain you make with your dog: your care on one side of the scale, his complete idolatry on the other. Not quite a fair bargain, but we humans, unlike our dogs, are seldom completely fair and unselfish.

Good husbandry pays off in dollars and cents too, particularly if you have more than one or two dogs, or run a semicommercial kennel. Clean, well-cared for dogs are most often healthy dogs, free from parasitic invaders and the small ills that bring other and greater woes in their wake. Good feeding and proper exercise help build strength and resistance to disease, and a sizable run keeps your canine friend from wandering into the path of some speeding car. Veterinarian bills and nursing time are substantially reduced, saving you money and time, when your dog is properly cared for.

Cleanliness, that partner to labor which is owned by some to be next to Godliness, is the first essential of good dog care. This applies to the dog's surrounding environment as well as to the dog himself. If your Basset sleeps in the house, provide him with a draft-free spot for his bed, away from general household traffic. This bed can be a piece of rug or a well-padded dog mattress. It doesn't particularly matter what material is used as long as it is kept clean and put in the proper place.

Feeding has been comprehensively discussed in the previous chapter, but the utensils used and the methods of feeding come more specifically under the heading of general care, so we will repeat these few facts mentioned in the previous chapter. Heavy aluminium feeding pans are best, since they are easily cleaned and do not chip as does agate or porcelain. Feed your dog regularly in the same place and at the same time. Establish a friendly and quiet atmosphere during feeding periods and do not coax him to eat. If he refuses the food or nibbles at it sparingly, remove his food and do not feed again until the next feeding period. Never allow a pan of food to stand before a healthy dog for more than thirty minutes under any circumstances. Should your Basset's appetite continue to be off, consult your veterinarian for the cause.

If you are feeding several dogs in an outside kennel, it is good practice to remain until all are finished, observing their appetites and eating habits while you wait. Often two dogs, kenneled together and given the same amount and kind of food, show different results. One will appear thin and the other in good condition. Sometimes the reason is a physiological one, but more often observation will show that the thinner dog is a slower eater than his kennel mate; that the latter dog gulps down his own food and then drives the thin dog away from his food pan before his ration is fully consumed and finishes this extra portion, too.

Never, never, force feed a healthy dog simply because he refuses an occasional meal. Force feeding and coaxing make finicky eaters and a finicky feeder is never in good coat or condition and turns feeding time into the most exasperating experience of the day. Rather than forcing or coaxing, it is better to starve your dog, showing no sympathy at all when he refuses food. If he is healthy, he will soon realize that he will experience hunger unless he eats when the food pan is put before him and will soon develop a normal and healthy appetite. Immediately upon removing the food pans, they should be thoroughly washed and stacked, ready for the next mealtime

During hot weather, be certain that your dog has a constant supply of fresh, clean water. In winter, water left outside in runs will freeze solid and be of no use to the dogs, so it is best to provide fresh water two or three times a day and remove the pail after the dogs have had their fill. Always provide water within an hour after feeding.

It has been the experience of most dog people that animals kept or kenneled outdoors, both winter and summer, are healthier and in better condition generally than their softer living housedog brethren. Light and the seasons have a great deal to do with shedding and coat condition. The outdoor dog, living in an environment approaching the natural, has regular shedding periods, after which his new coat comes in hard, strong, and glossy. Housedogs living in conditions of artificial light and heat seem to shed constantly, and seldom possess the good coat exhibited by the dog who lives outdoors. The housedog is much more susceptible to quick changes in temperature, particularly in the winter when he is brought from a warm, furnace-heated house into the frigid out-of-doors. Never forget that your Basset is a sporting dog, not a lap dog, and treat him accordingly.

PLANNING YOUR RUN

Even the housedog should be provided with an outside run and house, a domain of his own to keep him in the sun and air and protect him from disturbance by children or other dogs. There, in his run, he is safe from accident, and you know he can't run away to become lost, strayed, or stolen. There, also, you can be sure he is not soiling or digging in your neighbor's newly planted lawn, a situation which can strain, to put it mildly, any "good neighbor policy." Provide shade in some section of the run against the hot summer sun. Natural shade from trees is the ideal, of course, but artificial shade can be provided by a canvas overthrow placed strategically.

The run should be as large as your property will permit. Six by fifteen feet is a good size for one to four dogs, but if space permits it, a longer run is preferable. If you are building a kennel of several runs, remember that the length is more important than the width, and connecting runs in a row can be cut down in width if the length provided is ample.

The best surface for your run is a question open for argument. Some breeders prefer packed-down fine cinders for their run surface, claiming that this material provides good drainage and is the best surface for a dog's feet, keeping them compact and strong. Actually, heredity and, to a lesser degree, diet, are the prime factors that produce good feet in dogs, but a dog's feet will spread and lose compactness if he is kept constantly on a soft or muddy surface. Cinders do make an excellent run, but this surface also makes an admirable place in which parasitic eggs and larvae can exist and thrive, and they are almost impossible to clean out from such a surface, short of resorting to a blowtorch. Others favor cement runs. They are easy to clean and present a good appearance. But again, we have a porous surface in which the minute eggs of parasites can take refuge. Only by daily scrubbing with a strong disinfectant, or periodic surface burning, can concrete runs be kept free of parasitic eggs and larvae.

Gravel and plain dirt runs present the same disadvantage, plus the difficulty of efficiently gathering stools from such surfaces. Dirt runs also become muddy in rainy weather and dusty in dry weather, making it necessary to change bedding often, and producing, as formerly mentioned, a deleterious effect upon the animal's feet. It would seem, then, that none of these run surfaces is the perfect answer to our problem. But there is yet another run surface which can give us better control over parasitic reinfestation. On this run we employ washed builders' sand for the surface. The dog generally defecates in a limited area, almost always at the end of his run farthest from the run door and his own house. Stools can easily be removed from the sand surface, and by digging down and removing one or two inches of sand below the stool, parasitic invaders are also removed. Fresh sand is filled into the spaces left by cleaning. The sand soon packs down and becomes a solid surface. The grains drop easily from the dog's feet and are not carried into his house to soil his bedding. This sand is not expensive, and periodically the whole surface can be removed and fresh sand brought in and leveled. An ideal run would be one with a cement base which can be washed down with disinfectants or a strong borax solution (which will destroy hookworm larvae) whenever the surface sand is completely removed and before a fresh sand surface is provided.

BUILDING YOUR RUN

If you plan to build the run yourself, you might consider the "soil-cement" surface as a base rather than true cement. Soil-cement is a subsurface employed on light-traffic airfields and many suburban roads; it is inexpensive, durable, and easily built without special knowledge or equipment. First remove the sod on the area to be converted into a run, then loosen the soil to a depth of about four inches with a spade and pulverize the soil, breaking up any lumps with a rake. Scatter dry cement at the rate of two-thirds of a sack of cement to a square yard of surface and mix in thoroughly with the soil until the mixture has a floury texture. Adjust your hose to a mist spray and water the surface until the soil-cement mixture will mold under pressure, and not crumble. Follow by raking the entire mixture to full depth to assure uniform moisture, and level at the same time. Now you must work quickly, compacting the run with a tamper and then rolling with a garden roller. All this must be done within a half-hour or the surface will harden while still uneven. After rolling, the surface should be smooth and even. Mist-spray again, then cover with a coating of damp sawdust or soil for a week, after which the run can be used. Remember to keep a slight slope on all run surfaces so that water can drain off without puddling. Soil-cement is also excellent for paths around, or to and from, the kennels.

CLEANING YOUR RUN

In removing stools from a run, never rake them together first. This practice tends to spread worm eggs over a greater area. Shovel each stool up separately and deposit it in a container. When the run is clean, carry the container to a previously prepared pit, dump the contents, and cover with a layer of dirt. Hose out the container and apply disinfectant, and

Ch. Santana-Mandeville's Just Fred.

the job is done with a minimum of bother. In winter, due to snow and ice, very little can be done about run sanitation. But those who live in climates which have definite and varied seasons have the consolation of knowing that worm eggs do not incubate nor fleas develop during cold weather. Therefore they must only do whatever is possible in run cleanliness for the sake of appearance and to keep down odors.

FENCING YOUR RUN

Fencing the run is our next problem. The ideal fencing is heavy chain link with metal supporting posts set in cement, and erected by experts. But if your pocketbook cries at such an expenditure (and the cost is not

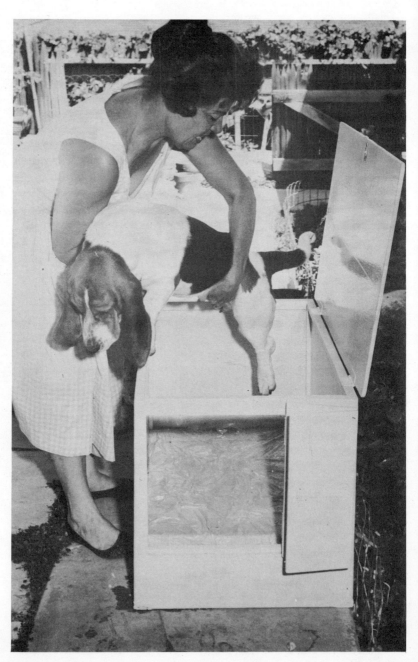

A clever combination of both a dog house and
bed for your Basset.

small), you can do your own fencing, cutting the cost drastically by purchasing cheaper wire, using cedar posts for supports, and girding your loins for a bit of labor. Hog wire, $1\frac{1}{2}''$ fox wire, or heavy poultry wire all can be used. Whatever fencing you employ, be sure it is high enough and is of a heavy enough gauge to be substantial. Dig post holes, using horizontally stretched string as a guide to keep them evenly in line, and dig them deeply enough to hold the posts securely. Leave approximately six feet of space between each post hole. Paint the section of the post which is to be buried in the hole with creosote or some other good wood preservative and set the posts in the holes. Concrete and rock, poured into the hole around the post, will provide a firm base. A horizontal top rail strengthens the run materially and will make for a better job. Brace all corner and gate posts as shown in the illustration. When your posts are in and set, borrow a wire stretcher for use in applying the wire fencing to the posts. This handy instrument can make the difference between a poor and a good job.

YOUR DOG HOUSE

The dog house can be simple or elaborate, reaching the extremes from a barrel set on cement blocks to a miniature human dwelling, complete with shingles and windows. The best kind of house comes somewhere in between these two extremes. Build the house large enough, with sleeping quarters approximately 3 by 2 feet, and 2 feet high at the highest point. Incorporate a front porch $1\frac{1}{2}$ feet deep on the front of the house. If the house is correctly situated, the porch roof offers shade from the sun and the porch itself a place to lie in rainy or snowy weather. Make the skeleton framework of one by twos, first building the two side sections, allowing three inches of extra height on the uprights for floor elevation. Incorporate the porch size in the over-all length of the side pieces and remember the back slope over the sleeping portion, which will accommodate the hinged roof.

Next build the floor frame and cover it with three-eighths-inch outdoor plywood, or tongue and groove siding. Cover the sides with the same material you use for the floor. If you allow your two-by-three-inch framing to show on the outside of the house, you will have a smooth inner surface to attach your floor platform to. Keep the floor the three inches above ground level provided by your side uprights and brace the floor by nailing three-inch pieces under the floor and to the inside bottom of the side uprights. Frame in the door section between the porch and the sleeping quarters, framing for a door up from the floor to hold in the bedding. Nail your plywood or tongue and groove siding over this framework, of course leaving the opening for the door, and nail the same wood across the back and the porch roof, thus closing the house in all around except for the roof section over the sleeping quarters. Build this section separately, with an overlay on the two sides and the back. Attach an underneath flange of wood on both sides and the rear, in from the edges, so that the flanges will fit snugly along the three outside edges of the house proper to keep out drafts and cold. Hinge this roof section to the back edge of the porch roof and cover the entire roof part with shingles or heavy tar paper, with a separate flap stripped along and covering the hinged edge. Paint the house (blue or blue-gray paint is said to discourage flies), and it is finished.

If you wish, you may insulate with board insulation on the inside, or double flooring can be provided with insulating paper between the layers. In cold weather a gunny sack or a piece of canvas, rug or blanket should be tacked at the top edge of the doorway to fall across the opening, thus blocking out cold air. If the house is big enough, an inside partial wall can be provided at one side of the door, essentially dividing the inner portion into a front hall with a weather-blocking partition between this hall and the sleeping quarters. If you build the house without the porch, you will find it necessary to build a separate platform on which the dog

A good spray to eliminate fleas, ticks, and lice should be a part of your grooming apparatus.

can lie outside in the sun after snow or rain. Should your ambitions embrace a full-sized kennel building with office, etc., it might be wise to investigate the prefabricated kennel buildings which are now on the market.

This house that you build, because of its size, is not an easy thing to handle or carry, so we suggest that you build it as close to the site you have picked for it as possible. The site should be at the narrow end of the run, with just a few inches of the porch jutting into the run and the greater bulk of the house outside of the run proper. Situate the house at the door end of the run, so that when you approach the run, the dog will not track through his excreta, which will be distributed at the end of the run farthest from the door. Try to set the house with its side to the north and back to the west. This gives protection from the coldest compass point in winter and shades the porch in summer from the hot afternoon sun.

Remember that the smaller and lower you can build your house without cramping your dog, the warmer it will be in the winter. If the house is not too large, is well built, and the doorway blocked adequately, you will be surprised by the amount of heat the dog's body will generate in cold weather to keep his sleeping quarters warm. To house several dogs, the necessary number of houses can be built or, if you so wish, one house doubled in length, with a dividing partition and two doorways, to service two separate runs.

Bedding for the sleeping box can consist of marsh grass, oat, rye, or wheat straw, or wood, pine, or cedar shavings. The latter is said to discourage fleas and lice and possesses an aromatic odor. If any of the other materials are used, shake a liberal supply of flea powder in the bedding once a week or each time the bedding is changed. The bedding may be changed once a month, but should be changed more often in rainy or muddy weather. Old bedding should be burned so it will not become a breeding place for parasites. Periodically the dog house should be cleaned out, washed with soap and water and a good disinfectant, and aired with the hinged roof section propped open.

GROOMING

Grooming should be a pleasant experience and a time of silent and delightful communication between you and your dog. Try to find the time to groom your dog once every day. It should take only a few minutes of your time, except during the season of shedding. By removing dead hair, dust, and skin scales in the daily grooming, you keep your Basset's coat glossy, his appearance neat. This kind of daily grooming also elimi-

Cut off the long, extra muzzle whiskers using
taped-end scissors to avoid injury should he move.

nates the necessity for frequent bathings. Go over the dog with a wire (or hound) grooming glove and finish with a stiff-bristled brush. The preparation, grooming and beautifying your dog for show ring competition is completely covered in the chapter headed Training Your Basset For the Show Ring, which chapter also will tell you all you want to know about entering your dog and the meaning of the various dog show classes.

Your Basset has a problem in this category peculiarly its own. I refer to the accumulation of food on the ends of its ears after feeding, or the soaked ends after drinking. To eliminate these problems the water dish should be deep and narrow so that the dog's ears hang on either side of it instead of in it. The food pan can be shaped the same for the same reason, or you can use an ordinary food pan and clean the ends of your Basset's ears after feeding. Most Bassets clean their own ears after feeding, flipping the ends toward their mouths and licking them clean. But it is best to clean them yourself. An accumulation of stale food on the ends of a dog's ears is certainly not desirable.

BATHING

You may bathe your dog or puppy any time you think it necessary, as long as you do not think it is necessary too frequently. Be careful in chilly weather to bathe him in a warm room and make sure he is completely dry before you allow him to venture out into the cold outdoors. When you bathe your dog, you soak him down to the skin and remove the protective oils from his coat. When a dog is exposed to rain and snow, the dampness is shed by the outer coat and kept from the skin by his undercoat. Therefore he is not likely to be affected by natural seasonal conditions. Be careful, however, that he is not exposed to these same conditions directly after a bath, as there is danger of his contracting a cold. During the time of shedding, a bath once a week is not too often if the weather is warm. It helps to remove loose hair and skin scales, as does the grooming that should follow the bath when the dog is completely dry. As mentioned above, your dog's coat is water-resistant, so the easiest way to insure the removal of deep dirt and odors caused by accumulated sebum is by employing a chemicalized liquid soap with a coconut-oil base. Some commercial dog soaps contain vermin poisons, but an occasional prepared vermicidal dip, after bathing and rinsing, is more effective and very much worth while. When bathing, rub the lather in strongly down to the skin, being careful not to get soap in the dog's eyes. Cover every inch of him with heavy lather, rub it in, scrape the excess of with your hands, rinse and

For show purposes the end of the Basset's tail is trimmed along with other jutting or uneven hair.

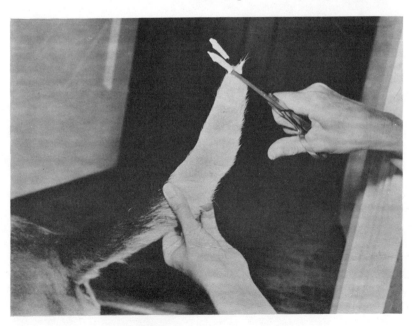

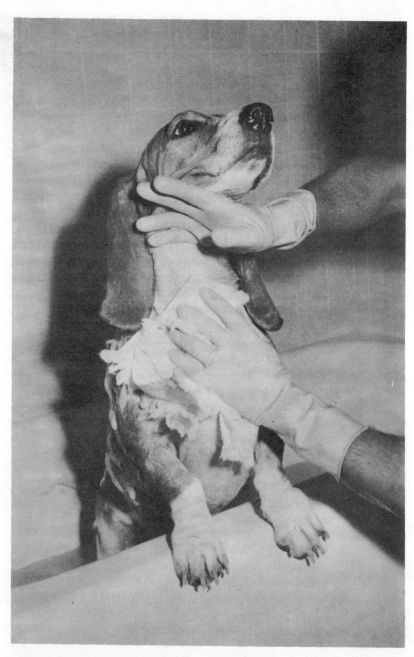

Many people are allergic to the tar oils or
chemicals in medicated rinses, so wear rubber
gloves.

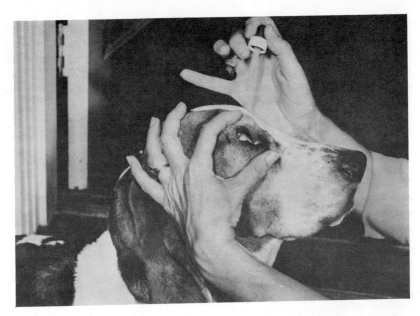

A few drops of light oil in the dog's eyes before bathing helps protect the eyes from excess soap.

On warm days dry your basset and massage loose hair off in the sunshine.

dry thoroughly, then walk him in the sun until he is ready for grooming. There are paste soaps available that require no rinsing, making the bathing of your Basset that much easier, or you may wish to use liquid detergents manufactured specifically for canine bathing. Prepared canned lathers, as well as dry shampoos, are all available at pet shops and are all useful in keeping your dog clean and odorless.

If your dog has walked in tar which you find you cannot remove by bathing, you can remove it with kerosene. The kerosene should be quickly removed with strong soap and water if it is not to burn and irritate the skin. Paint can be washed off with turpentine, which must also be quickly removed for the same reasons. Some synthetic paints, varnishes, enamels, and other like preparations, which are thinned with alcohol, can be removed by the same vehicle. If the paint (oil base) is close to the skin, linseed oil will dissolve it without irritation. Should your Basset engage in a tête-à-tête with a skunk, wash him immediately (if you can get near him) with soap and hot water, or soak him with tomato juice if you can find enough available, then walk him in the hot sun. The odor evaporates most quickly under heat.

A box of small sticks with cotton-tipped ends, which are manufactured under various brand names, are excellent for cleaning your Basset's ears. Drop into the ear a mixture of ether and alcohol, or of propylene glycol, to dissolve dirt and wax, then swab the ear clean with the cotton-tipped stick. Surplus liquid will quickly evaporate.

CARE OF NAILS AND TEETH

Keep your dog's nails trimmed short. Overgrown nails cause lameness, foot ailments, spread toes, and hare feet. If your dog does a great deal of walking on cement, nail growth is often kept under control naturally by wearing off on the cement surface. To accomplish this task with the least possible trouble, use a nail-cutter specifically designed for use on dogs and cut away only the horny dead section. If you cut too deeply, you will cause bleeding. A flashlight held under the nail will enable you to see the dark area of the blood line so you can avoid cutting into it. If you should tap the blood supply in the nail don't be overly alarmed, simply keep the dog quiet until the severed capillaries close and the bleeding stops. Munsel's solution or a styptic pencil applied to the bleeding nail helps to hurry coagulation. After you have cut the nails, file them smooth with the use of a nail file. File from above with a downward, rounding stroke. If a nail has bled from trimming, do not file it for at least twenty-four hours.

Artificial bones given twice a week will help prevent tartar from form-

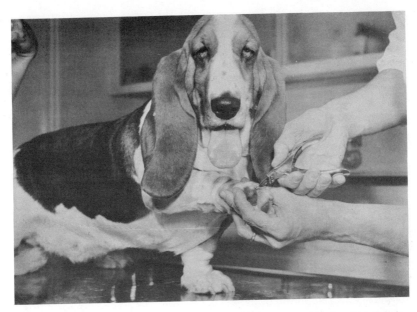

Keep your Basset's nails clipped down.
Overgrown nails cause lameness. Use a guillotine
clipper.

During grooming, check teeth for cleaning.

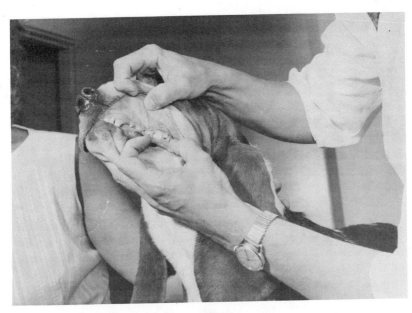

ing on your dog's teeth. His teeth pierce the bones, scraping off tooth residue in the process, keeping his teeth clean and white. If tartar should form, it can be chipped off with the same kind of instrument your dentist uses on your teeth for that purpose, or your veterinarian can clean them efficiently and without bother to you. Check your dog's mouth every other week for broken, loose, or abscessed teeth, particularly when he has passed his prime. Bad teeth must be tended by your veterinarian before they affect your dog's general health.

FLIES

During the summer months certain flies, commonly called "deer" flies, bite at the ears causing great discomfort, the formation of scabs, subsequent baldness, and sometimes infection in that area. A good liquid insecticide, one of the many recently developed for fly control, should be rubbed or sprayed on the dog's ears as often as necessary to keep these pests away. Skin-disease salve which contains sulphur and oil of turpentine as a vehicle is also efficacious against flies, particularly if D.D.T. flea powder is shaken on top of the salve, where it adheres, giving extra protection. Oil of Benzoin and oil of Cade, painted on the ears, are also effective.

RATS

If rats invade the kennel area, they should be eradicated as quickly as possible. Not only are they disease carriers, but they are an affront to our more delicate senses. To get rid of them, set out small pans of dog meal near their holes every night for several nights until you have them coming to these pans to feed. Then mix Red Squill with the dog food they are being fed, eight measures of dog meal to one of Red Squill. After a single night's feeding of this poisonous mixture, you will generally rid your premises of these gray marauders. Red Squill is a drug that is non-poisonous to all animals except rodents, so it can be used around the kennel with safety.

TRAVEL

When traveling in hot weather with your dog, never leave him in a closed car in the sun alone. Death takes its grisly toll each summer of dogs so treated. Carry his water pail and food dish with you and take care of his needs as you do your own when on the road. If you intend changing his diet to one more easily fed when traveling, begin the change

Puppies should be dried with mechanical dryer
to avoid colds. Remember he is soaked to skin.

a few days before your trip so he can become accustomed to it. Gaines Research Division publishes a list of approximately 3,500 hostelries across the country that will accept dogs—a handy booklet for the dog-loving traveler to have.

If you find it necessary to ship a Basset to another section of the country, make sure the crate you use is large enough in all dimensions to keep the dog from being cramped during his journey. Check to see that there are no large openings or weak sections which might break in transit and allow the dog's limbs to project out of the crate. Consult your veterinarian or your local express agency for data on state health certificates. Supply the dog with a pan, rigidly attached to the crate, for water, and throw a few dog biscuits on the floor of the crate for the dog to gnaw during his journey to alleviate boredom. Be sure there are air holes in strategic locations to provide air and ventilation. If possible, the top surface of

Three basically colored Bassets are exhibited as
Susan Harris takes a brace for a stroll in the
Californian sunshine.

the crate should be rounded, rather than flat, to discourage the parking
of other crates on top of the dog crate. Strips of wood, nailed horizontally
along the outside of the crate and projecting out from the surface, will
prevent adjacent crates, or boxes, from being jammed tightly against the
dog crate and thus blocking and defeating the purpose of the ventilation
holes.

A periodic health check of your Basset by your veterinarian can pay big
mental and monetary dividends. When you take him for his examination,
remember to bring with you samples of his stool and urine for analysis.

EXERCISE

Your Basset needs a good deal of exercise if he is to be in good physical
shape and not become fat. The hunting Basset generally has enough and
the right kind of exercise if he is used consistently during the hunting
season. At other times many field Bassets are allowed to hunt by themselves, the theory being that it keeps them keen and any bad form they

may develop can be corrected. The exercise they get from this is certainly worthwhile and beneficial.

The show dog of course needs lots of good exercise to keep his flesh and muscles tight, his gait swinging and his eyes bright. Throwing a ball or a stick for him to retrieve is ideal exercise coupled with nice long walks. This will also be of benefit to you for most of us tend to eat too much and exercise too little.

The owner of the pet dog should be just as attentive to this facet of canine husbandry. Even though your Basset is not a gun dog or a show dog, he still needs adequate exercise to continue being a good pet and companion. Without exercise he will become fat and lazy and not as capable of combating disease. The same kind of exercise recommended for the show dog is fine for the pet dog too.

We have considered in this chapter the elements of physical care, but we must not forget that your Basset needs mental care as well. His character and mental health need nourishment, grooming, and exercise, just as much as his physical being. Give him your companionship and understanding, teach him right from wrong, and treat him as you would a friend whom you enjoy associating with. This, too, is a part of his general care, and perhaps the most important part for both you and your dog.

Remember that good general care is the first and most important part of canine ownership and disease prevention. The health and happiness of your Basset is in your hands. A small amount of labor each day by those hands is your dog's health and life insurance, and the premium is paid by your Basset in love and devotion.

Ch. Slippery Hill Quixote, shown here winning
the Rancocas Basset Hound Club Specialty Show
in 1970.

CHAPTER VII

The Brood Bitch

If we want to succeed in improvement within our breed, we must have an even greater trueness to breed type in our bitches than we have in their breeding partners. The productive value of the bitch is comparatively limited in scope by seasonal vagary and this, in turn, increases the importance of every litter she produces.

To begin breeding, we must of necessity begin with a bitch as the foundation. The foundation of all things must be strong and free from faults, or the structure we build upon it will crumble. The bitch we choose for our foundation bitch must, then, be a good bitch, as fine as we can possibly acquire, not in structure alone, but in mentality and character as well. She is a product of her germ plasm, and this most important facet of her being must be closely analyzed so that we can compensate, in breeding, for her hidden faults. Structurally, the good brood bitch should be strongly made and up to standard size. She should be deep and not too long in body, for overlong bitches are generally too long in loin and weak in back, and after a litter tend to sag in back line. She must possess good bone strength throughout, yet she should not be so coarse as to lack femininity. Weakness and delicacy are not the essence of femininity in our breed and should be particularly avoided in the brood bitch.

THE PERIOD OF HEAT

Your bitch will first come in season when she is between seven and eleven months of age. Though this is an indication that nature considers her old enough and developed enough to breed, it is best to allow her to pass this first heat and plan to breed her when she next comes in season. This should come within six months if her environment remains the same. Daylight, which is thought to affect certain glands, seems to occasionally influence the ratio of time between heats, as will complete change in environment. Scientific studies of the incidence of seasonal variation in the mating cycles of bitches indicates that more bitches come in heat and are bred during the months of February through May than at any other time of year. The figures might not be completely reliable, since they were assembled through birth registrations in the A.K.C., and many breeders refrain from fall and winter breedings so they will not have winter or early spring litters.

Some breeders claim a bitch should not be bred until she has passed two seasons, but it is not necessary to wait this long. In fact, should you breed your bitch at her second season, it will probably be better for her, settling her in temperament and giving her body greater maturity and grace.

When your bitch is approaching her period of heat and you intend to breed her, have her stool checked for intestinal parasites, and if any are present, worm her. Feed her a well-balanced diet, such as she should have been getting all along. Her appetite will increase in the preparatory stage of the mating cycle as her vulva begins to swell. She will become restless, will urinate more frequently, and will allow dogs to approach her, but will not allow copulation. Within the bitch other changes are taking place at this stage. Congestion begins in the reproductive tract, the horns of the uterus and the vagina thicken, and the luteal bodies leave the ovaries.

The first sign of blood from the vulva ushers in the second stage of the mating cycle. In some bitches no blood appears at all, or so little that it goes unnoticed by the owner, and sometimes we find a bitch who will bleed throughout the cycle. In either circumstances we must depend upon other signs. The bitch becomes very playful with animals of her own and the opposite sex, but will still not permit copulation. This is, of course, a condition which is very trying to male dogs with which she comes in contact. Congestion within the bitch reaches a high point during this

REPRODUCTIVE SYSTEM OF THE BITCH
1. Vulva   2. Anus   3. Rectum   4. Uterus
5. Kidney   6. Ovary   7. Ribs (indicated)
8. Developing embryo   9. Vagina

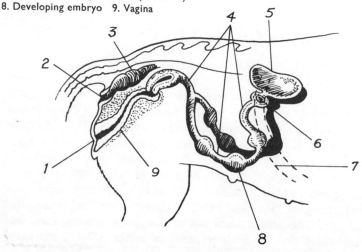

period. Ova develop within the follicles of the ovaries, and, normally, the red discharge gradually turns to pink, becoming lighter in color until it becomes straw color and is no longer obvious. Her vulva is more swollen, and she becomes increasingly more playful with males. This period is generally of about ten days' duration, but the time varies greatly with the individual. Rather than rely upon any set time period, it is best to conclude that this period reaches its conclusion when the bitch will stand for the stud and permit copulation. This generally occurs at about the tenth day, but can take place as early as the fourth or fifth day of this period or as late as the seventeenth day.

The third period in the cycle is the acceptance period. The bitch will swing her hind end toward the dog, her tail will arch up and stand high, and she will permit copulation. Sometimes the stud may have to tease her for a time, but she will eventually give in. The bitch may be sensitive and yelp and pull away when the stud's penis touches the lining of the vagina. If this occurs several times, it is best to wait another day, until the sensitivity has left this region. A very definite indication that the bitch is in the acceptance period is the softness and flaccidity of the vulva, from which the firmness and congestion has gone. Within the bitch the ovarian follicles have been growing ever bigger, and approximately midway in the acceptance period, some of them burst and the eggs are ready for fertilization. If the bitch has a normal mating cycle, as shown on the diagram, the best time to breed her is about the thirteenth or fourteenth day of the mating cycle, when ovulation has occurred. This time also varies with the individual bitch, so that until you have bred your bitch

BREEDING CYCLE OF THE BITCH

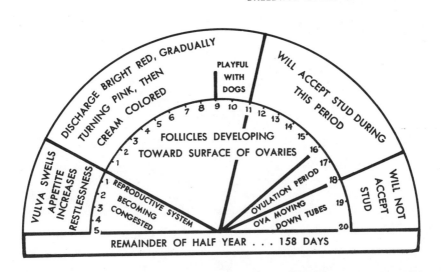

Ch. Santana Mandeville Ichabod
when he was ten months old.

once or twice and feel that you know the best time for her, it is better to breed her on the eleventh day and every other day thereafter until her period of acceptance is over. This last, of course, is generally only possible when the stud is owned by you. One good breeding is actually all that is necessary to make your bitch pregnant, providing that breeding is made at the right time. If copulation is forced before the bitch is ready, the result is no conception or a small litter, since the sperm must wait for ovulation and the life of the sperm is limited. The acceptance period ceases rather abruptly, and is signaled by the bitch's definite resistance to male advances.

HANDLING THE MATING

If your bitch is a maiden, it is best to breed her this first time to an older stud who knows his business. When you bring her to the stud and if there are adjoining wire-enclosed runs, put the stud in one run and the bitch in the adjacent one. They will make overtures through the wire and later, when the stud is loosed in the run with the bitch, copulation generally occurs quickly. You may have to hold the bitch if she is flighty or reluctant, sometimes a problem with maiden bitches. If your bitch fails to conceive from a good and proper breeding, do not immediately put the blame on the stud. In most instances it is the fault of either the bitch or the owner of the bitch, who has not adequately timed the mating. Many bitch owners fail to recognize the first signs of the mating cycle and so bring their bitch to the stud either too early or too late. Normal physiology of the reproductive system can be interrupted or delayed by disturbance, disease, or illness in any part of the dog's body. A sick bitch will therefore generally not come in season, though it is time to do so, until after she has completely recovered and returned to normal. Bitches past their prime and older tend to have a shorter mating cycle and so must be bred sooner than usual to assure pregnancy.

During copulation and the resulting tie, you should assist the stud dog owner as much as possible. If the stud evidences pain when he attempts to force his penis in the vulva, check the bitch. In virgin bitches you may find a web of flesh which runs vertically across the vaginal opening and causes pain to the dog when his penis is forced against it. This web must be broken by hooking your finger around it and pulling if a breeding is to be consummated. After the tense excitement of the breeding and while the tie is in effect, speak to the bitch quietly and keep her from moving until the tie is broken, then snap a leash onto her collar and take her for a fast walk around the block without pausing. After that she can be taken home in the car. If it is necessary to travel any great distance before she

Before attempting a breeding, allow the stud and
the bitch to become acquainted. This initial
introduction can also be accomplished through
adjoining runs.

Fractious bitch may need muzzling before
breeding.

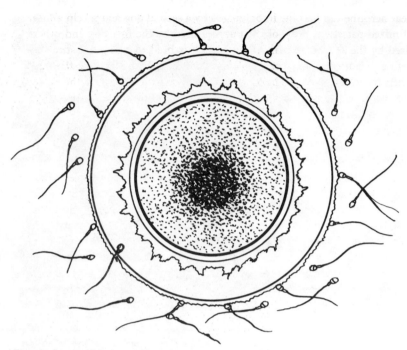

The egg is a special giant cell produced by the
ovaries of the bitch. It is shown here being
assaulted by sperm. The dark nucleus is the seat
of the chromosomes. The nucleus is surrounded
by growth enzymes.

arrives again in familiar surroundings, it is best to allow her a period of
quiet rest before attempting the journey.

FALSE PREGNANCY

Occasionally fertile bitches, whether bred or not, will have false preg-
nancies and show every physical manifestation of true gestation up to the
last moment. In some cases a bitch may be truly bred and then, after a
month, resorb her fetuses. The only way of differentiating between
psuedo-pregnancy and fetal resorbtion is by palpation, or feeling with the
hands, to locate the fetal lump in the uterus. This is a difficult task for
one who has not had vast experience.

PRENATAL CARE

After you have returned home with your bitch, do not allow any males near her. She can become impregnated by a second dog and whelp a litter of mixed paternity, some of the puppies sired by the first dog and others sired by the second animal. Often a bitch is bred to a selected stud just before ovulation. The sperm will live long enough to fertilize the eggs when they flush down. The next day, another male breeds to the bitch, the sperm of the two dogs mix within her and both become sires of the resulting litter.

Let us assume that your bitch is in good health and you have had a good breeding to the stud of your choice at the proper time in the bitch's mating cycle to insure pregnancy. The male sperm fertilizes the eggs and life begins. From this moment on you will begin to feed the puppies which will be born in about sixty to sixty-three days from ovulation. Every bit of food you give the bitch is nutritionally aiding in the fetal development within her. Be sure that she is being provided with enough milk to supply calcium, meat for phosphorus and iron, and all the other essential vitamins and minerals. A vitamin and mineral supplement may be incorporated into the food if used moderately. Alfalfa leaf meal of 24 per cent protein content should become part of the diet. She must be fed well for her own

WHELPING BOX
Note the hinged side for easy cleaning and the step that aids the bitch laden with milk to enter easily. The guard rail keeps puppies that get behind the bitch from being crushed, and the extra length of the side posts provides for later adding of side boards.

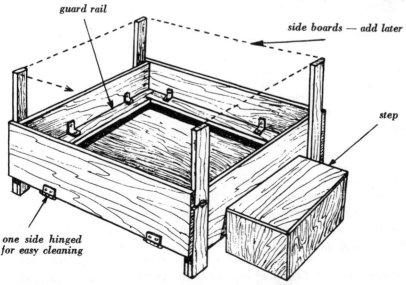

guard rail

side boards — add later

step

one side hinged
for easy cleaning

maintenance and for the development of the young *in utero*, particularly during the last thirty days of the gestation period. She should not, however, be given food to such excess that she becomes fat.

Your bitch, her run, and house or bed should be free of worm and flea eggs. She should be allowed a moderate amount of free exercise in the prenatal period to keep her from becoming fat and soft and from losing muscular tone and elasticity. If your bitch has not had enough exercise prior to breeding and you wish to harden and reduce her, accustom her to the exercise gradually and it will do her a great deal of good. But do not

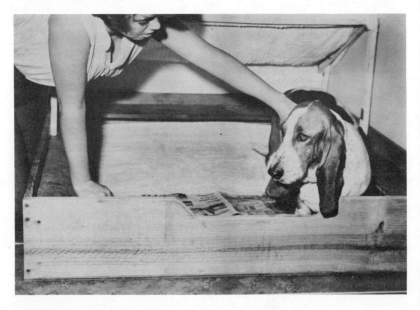

Pre-whelping care for the expectant mama includes making the bitch acquainted with, and at home in, the box in which she will subsequently whelp.

allow her to indulge in unaccustomed, abrupt, or violent exercise, or she might abort.

The puppies develop in the horns of the uterus, not in the "tubes" (Fallopian tubes), as is commonly thought. As the puppies develop, the horns of the uterus lengthen and the walls expand. A month before the bitch is due to whelp, incorporate fresh liver in her diet two or three times a week. This helps to keep her free from constipation and aids in the coming necessary production of milk for the litter. If the litter is going to be small, she will not show much sign until late in the gestation period. But if the litter is going to be a normal or large one, she will begin to show distention of the abdomen at about thirty-five days after the breeding. Her appetite will have been increasing during this time, and gradually the fact of her pregnancy will become more and more evident.

THE WHELPING BOX

Several days before she is due to whelp, the whelping box should be prepared. It should be located in a dimly lit area removed from disturbance by other dogs, or humans. The box should be about 36" square, enclosed on all sides by eight- to ten-inch high boards, either plank or plywood. Boards must be added above these in about three weeks to keep the pups from climbing out. Three inches up from the flooring (when it is packed down), a half by two-inch smooth wooden slat should be attached to the sides with small angle irons, all around as a rail, or a pipe rail can be used. This will prevent the bitch from accidentally squeezing to death any puppy which crawls behind her. On the floor of the box lay a smooth piece of rubber matting which is easily removed and cleaned when the bedding is cleaned or changed. The bedding itself should be of rye or oat straw, and enough of it supplied so that the bitch can hollow out a nest and still leave some of the nesting material under the pups. Another method much used is to have several layers of newspapers in the bottom of the box so that they can be removed one or two at a time as they become soiled during whelping. After the litter is completely whelped, the straw bedding is provided and hollowed into a saucer shape so the whelps will be kept together in a limited area. The whelping box should be raised from the ground and a smaller box or step provided, to make it easier for the bitch to enter or leave.

WHELPING THE LITTER

As the time approaches for the whelping, the bitch will become restless; she may refuse food and begin to make her nest. Her temperature will drop approximately one degree the day before she is ready to whelp, and she will show a definite dropping down through the abdomen. Labor begins with pressure from within that forces the puppies toward the pelvis. The bitch generally twists around as the puppy is being expelled to lick the fluid which accompanies the birth. Sometimes the sac surrounding the puppy will burst from pressure. If it doesn't, the puppy will be born in the sac, a thin, membranous material called the fetal envelope. The navel cord runs from the puppy's navel to the afterbirth, or placenta. If the bitch is left alone at whelping time, she will rip the fetal caul, bite off the navel cord and eat the sac, cord, and placenta. Should the cord be broken off in birth so that the placenta remains in the bitch, it will generally be expelled with the birth of the next whelp. After disposing of these items, the bitch will lick and clean the new puppy until the next one is about to be born, and the process will then repeat itself. Under completely normal circumstances, your bitch is quite able to whelp her litter and look after them without any help from you, but since the whelping might not be normal, it is best for the breeder to be present, particularly so in the case of bitches who are having their first litter.

If the breeder is present, he or she can remove the sac, cut the umbilical cord, and gently pull on the rest of the cord, assuming that the placenta has not yet been ejected, until it is detached and drawn out. Some breeders keep a small box handy in which they place each placenta, so they can, when the whelping is completed, check them against the number of puppies to make sure that no placenta has been retained. The navel cord should be cut about three inches from the pup's belly. The surplus will dry up and drop off in a few days. There is no need to tie it after cutting. You need not attempt to sterilize your hands or the implements you might use in helping the bitch to whelp, since the pups will be practically surrounded with bacteria of all kinds, some benign and others which they are born equipped to combat.

If a bitch seems to be having difficulty in expelling a particularly large puppy, you can help by wrapping a towel around your hands to give you purchase, grasping the partly expelled whelp, and gently pulling. Do not pull too hard, or you might injure the pup. The puppies can be born either head first or tail first. Either way is normal. As the pups are born, the sac broken, and the cord snipped, dry them gently but vigorously with a towel and put them at the mother's breast, first squeezing some milk to the surface and then opening their mouths for the entrance of the teat. You may have to hold them there by the head until they begin sucking.

Often several puppies are born in rapid succession, then an interval of time may elapse before another one is born. If the bitch is a slow whelper and seems to be laboring hard after one or more pups have been born, regular injections of Pitocin, at three-hour intervals, can help her in delivery. Pituitrin is a similar drug and the one most often used, though Pitocin brings less nausea and directly affects the uterus. Both these drugs should be administered hypodermically into the hind leg of the bitch at the rear of the thigh. After the bitch has seemingly completed her whelping, it is good practice to administer another shot of the drug to make sure no last pup, alive or dead, is still unborn and to cause her to clean out any residue left from the whelping. Never use either of these drugs until she has whelped at least one pup.

Allow her to rest quietly and enjoy the new sensation of motherhood for several hours, then insist that she leave her litter, though she won't want to, and take her out to relieve herself. Offer her some warm milk. From then on, feed her as recommended during the gestation period, with the addition of three milk feedings per day. Sometimes milk appears in the udders before birth, but generally it comes in when the pups begin to nurse, since it is manufactured by glands, from blood, while the pups are at the breast.

Now is the time to cull the litter. Of course, all young which are not

After the bitch has whelped her litter, the newborn pups must be watched closely, and any not getting enough to eat must be manually helped.

normal should be culled immediately at birth. If the bitch whelps six or less pups and all seem strong and healthy, no culling is required. If she has a particularly large litter, it does not pay, in the long run, to raise all the whelps. Allow her to keep five or six of the best and sturdiest and cull the rest. Those which you have retained will grow better and be larger and stronger than if you allowed the entire large litter to live. Quiet puppies are healthy ones. Constant crying and squirming of the pups is a danger signal, and a check should be made to see what ails them. It may be that the bitch is not providing enough milk and they are hungry, or perhaps they are cold. Sometimes the trouble is parasitic infection, or

Lady Matilda Le Soubrette and her fine litter,
owned by Mr. and Mrs. L. R. Cummings.

A Basset matron during the nursing period.

possibly coccidiosis, or navel infection. Dr. Walter Koch, in 1950, at the University of Munich, Animal Institute, reported a bacillus, *Aerogenes,* which he claimed caused many deaths of young puppies. This bacillus infects from contact with the dam's rectum. It multiplies rapidly in the whelp's intestines, and the normal bacillus in the stomach and intestines seems to have no effect of the lethal bacillus. It begins with the first digestion of the pups and attacks the basic internal organs, exhibiting symptoms on the second or third day following birth. The pups develop cramps, fail to suck, whimper, and die within two or three days. The disease does

The proper method of handling a newly born
Basset puppy. The hands must carefully support it.

not seem to be contagious to other well puppies. If there is something wrong with the pups, whatever it may be, you need professional advice and should call your veterinarian immediately.

Except for the removal of dew claws the pups, if healthy, need not be bothered until it is time to begin their supplementary feeding at about three weeks. Dew claws should be removed on about the second day after birth. Puppies and their needs, dietary and otherwise, are discussed more fully in another chapter.

There are several ills which might befall the bitch during gestation and whelping which must be considered. Eclampsia, sometimes called

Newborn Basset pups cuddled up to keep warm.

milk fever, is perhaps most common. This is a metabolic disturbance brought on by a deficiency of calcium and phosphorus in the diet. If you give your bitch plenty of milk and a good diet such as we have recommended, she should not be troubled with this condition. Should your bitch develop eclampsia—evidenced by troubled shaking, wild expression, muscular rigidity, and a high temperature—it can be quickly relieved by an injection of calcium gluconate in the vein.

Should your bitch be bred by accident to an undesirable animal, your veterinarian can cause her to abort by the use of any one of several efficient canine abortifacients. He can also aid old bitches who have been resorbing their fetuses to carry them full term and whelp with the aid of stilbestrol.

Mastitis, an udder infection, is a chief cause of puppy deaths. It is generally mistaken by the uninformed for "acid milk," a condition which does not exist in dogs because the bitch's milk is naturally acid. Mastitis is an udder infection which cuts off part of the milk supply and the whelps either die of infection, contracted from the infected milk, or from starvation, due to the lack of sufficient milk. It is not necessary to massage the dam's breasts at weaning time with camphorated oil. They will cake naturally and quickly quit secreting milk if left completely alone.

Growths, infections, injuries, cysts, and other and various ailments can affect the female reproductive system and must be taken care of by your veterinarian. The great majority of bitches who have been well cared for and well fed are strong and healthy, and the bearing of litters is a natural procedure—the normal function of the female of the species to bear and rear the next generation, and in so doing fulfill her precious destiny.

PERPETUAL WHELPING CHART

	1	2	3	4	5	6	7	8	9	10	11	12	13	14	15	16	17	18	19	20	21	22	23	24	25	26	27	28	29	30	31
Bred—Jan.	1	2	3	4	5	6	7	8	9	10	11	12	13	14	15	16	17	18	19	20	21	22	23	24	25	26	27	28	29	30	31
Due—March	5	6	7	8	9	10	11	12	13	14	15	16	17	18	19	20	21	22	23	24	25	26	27	28	29	30	31	1	2	3	4
Bred—Feb.	1	2	3	4	5	6	7	8	9	10	11	12	13	14	15	16	17	18	19	20	21	22	23	24	25	26	27	28			
Due—April	5	6	7	8	9	10	11	12	13	14	15	16	17	18	19	20	21	22	23	24	25	26	27	28	29	30	1	2			
Bred—Mar.	1	2	3	4	5	6	7	8	9	10	11	12	13	14	15	16	17	18	19	20	21	22	23	24	25	26	27	28	29	30	31
Due—May	3	4	5	6	7	8	9	10	11	12	13	14	15	16	17	18	19	20	21	22	23	24	25	26	27	28	29	30	31	1	2
Bred—Apr.	1	2	3	4	5	6	7	8	9	10	11	12	13	14	15	16	17	18	19	20	21	22	23	24	25	26	27	28	29	30	
Due—June	3	4	5	6	7	8	9	10	11	12	13	14	15	16	17	18	19	20	21	22	23	24	25	26	27	28	29	30	1	2	
Bred—May	1	2	3	4	5	6	7	8	9	10	11	12	13	14	15	16	17	18	19	20	21	22	23	24	25	26	27	28	29	30	31
Due—July	3	4	5	6	7	8	9	10	11	12	13	14	15	16	17	18	19	20	21	22	23	24	25	26	27	28	29	30	31	1	2
Bred—June	1	2	3	4	5	6	7	8	9	10	11	12	13	14	15	16	17	18	19	20	21	22	23	24	25	26	27	28	29	30	
Due—August	3	4	5	6	7	8	9	10	11	12	13	14	15	16	17	18	19	20	21	22	23	24	25	26	27	28	29	30	31	1	
Bred—July	1	2	3	4	5	6	7	8	9	10	11	12	13	14	15	16	17	18	19	20	21	22	23	24	25	26	27	28	29	30	31
Due—September	2	3	4	5	6	7	8	9	10	11	12	13	14	15	16	17	18	19	20	21	22	23	24	25	26	27	28	29	30	1	2
Bred—Aug.	1	2	3	4	5	6	7	8	9	10	11	12	13	14	15	16	17	18	19	20	21	22	23	24	25	26	27	28	29	30	31
Due—October	3	4	5	6	7	8	9	10	11	12	13	14	15	16	17	18	19	20	21	22	23	24	25	26	27	28	29	30	31	1	2
Bred—Sept.	1	2	3	4	5	6	7	8	9	10	11	12	13	14	15	16	17	18	19	20	21	22	23	24	25	26	27	28	29	30	
Due—November	3	4	5	6	7	8	9	10	11	12	13	14	15	16	17	18	19	20	21	22	23	24	25	26	27	28	29	30	1	2	
Bred—Oct.	1	2	3	4	5	6	7	8	9	10	11	12	13	14	15	16	17	18	19	20	21	22	23	24	25	26	27	28	29	30	31
Due—December	3	4	5	6	7	8	9	10	11	12	13	14	15	16	17	18	19	20	21	22	23	24	25	26	27	28	29	30	31	1	2
Bred—Nov.	1	2	3	4	5	6	7	8	9	10	11	12	13	14	15	16	17	18	19	20	21	22	23	24	25	26	27	28	29	30	
Due—January	3	4	5	6	7	8	9	10	11	12	13	14	15	16	17	18	19	20	21	22	23	24	25	26	27	28	29	30	31	1	
Bred—Dec.	1	2	3	4	5	6	7	8	9	10	11	12	13	14	15	16	17	18	19	20	21	22	23	24	25	26	27	28	29	30	31
Due—February	2	3	4	5	6	7	8	9	10	11	12	13	14	15	16	17	18	19	20	21	22	23	24	25	26	27	28	1	2	3	4

Ch. Santana-Mandeville J. P. Morgan.
This fine specimen of the breed is recognized as
one of the top producers in the famous kennels.

CHAPTER VIII

The Stud Dog

If what we have said about the unrivaled importance of the brood bitch is true, it may be difficult to understand why we pay so much attention to the male lines of descent. The reason is that stud dogs tend to mold the aspects of the breed on the whole and in any given locality to a much greater extent than do brood bitches. While the brood bitch may control type in a kennel, the stud dog can control type over a much larger area. The truth of this can be ascertained by the application of simple mathematics.

Let us assume that the average litter is comprised of five puppies. The brood bitch will produce, then, a maximum of ten puppies a year. In that same year a popular, good producing, well-publicized stud dog may be used on the average of three times weekly (many name studs, in various breeds, have been used even more frequently over a period of several years). This popular stud can sire fifteen puppies a week, employing the figures mentioned above, or 780 puppies a year. Compare this total to the bitch's yearly total of ten puppies, and you can readily see why any one stud dog wields a much greater influence over the breed in general than does a specific brood bitch. Actually Basset stud dogs are sometimes lazy breeders and to use one consistently three times a week is a bit too often; once a week would still give us a total of 260 puppies a year.

GENERAL CARE OF THE STUD DOG

The care of the stud dog follows the same procedure as outlined in the chapter on general care. He needs a balanced diet, clean quarters, and plenty of exercise, but no special care as does the brood bitch. Though it is against most of the advice previously written on the subject, we recommend that the stud be used in breeding for the first time when he is about twelve months old. He is as capable of siring a litter of fine and healthy pups at this age as he ever will be. He should be bred to a steady, knowing bitch who has been bred before, and when she is entirely ready to accept him. Aid him if necessary this first time. See that nothing disturbs him during copulation. In fact, the object of this initial breeding is to see that all goes smoothly and easily. If you succeed in this aim, the young dog will be a willing and eager stud for the rest of his life, the kind of stud that it is a pleasure to own and use.

After this first breeding, use him sparingly until he has reached sixteen or seventeen months of age. After that, if he is in good health, there is no reason why he cannot be used reasonably during his best and most fertile years.

MALE REPRODUCTIVE ORGANS

The male organs vital for reproduction consist of a pair of each: testicles, where the sperm is produced; epididymis, in which the sperm are stored; and *vas deferens*, through which the sperm are transported. The dog possesses no seminal vesicle as does man. But, like man, the male dog is always in an active stage of reproduction and can be used at any time.

MECHANICS OF MATING

When the stud has played with the bitch for a short period and the bitch is ready, he will cover her. There is a bone in his penis, and behind this bone is a group of very sensitive nerves which cause a violent thrust reflex when pressure is applied. His penis, unlike most other animals', has a bulbous enlargement at its base. When the penis is thrust into the bitch's vagina, it goes through a muscular ring at the opening of the vagina. As it passes into the vagina, pressure on the reflex nerves causes a violent thrust forward, and the penis, and particularly the bulb, swells enormously, preventing withdrawal through the constriction band of the vulva. The stud ejaculates semen swarming with sperm, which is forced through the cervix, uterus, Fallopian tubes, and into the capsule which surrounds the ovaries, and the breeding is consummated.

The dog and bitch are tied, or "hung," and the active part of the breeding is completed. The owner of the bitch should then stand at her head and hold her by the collar. The stud's owner should kneel next to the animals with his hand or arm under the bitch's stomach, directly in front of her hindquarters, to prevent her from suddenly sitting while still tied. He should talk soothingly to the stud and gently prevent him from attempting to leave the bitch for a little while. Presently the stud owner should turn the dog around off the bitch's back by first lifting the front legs off and to the ground and then lifting one hind leg over the back of the bitch until dog and bitch are standing tail to tail, or side by side if the stud prefers.

Dogs remain in this position for various lengths of time after copulation, but fifteen minutes to a half an hour is generally average. When the congestion of blood leaves the penis, the bulb shrinks and the animals part.

The stud dog owner should keep a muzzle handy to be used on snappy

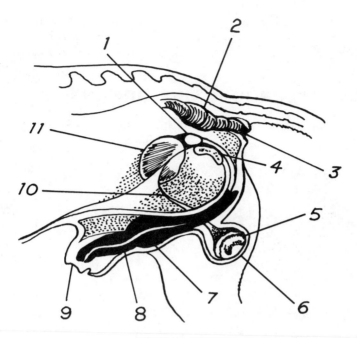

DIAGRAM OF MALE REPRODUCTIVE AND
ANAL SYSTEM
1. Prostate   2. Rectum   3. Site of anal glands
4. Section of pelvic bone   5. Testicle
6. Scrotum   7. Bulb (section of penis)
8. Peni   9. Sheath   10. Vas deferens   11. Bladder

bitches. Some virgin bitches, due to fright, may cause injury to the stud by biting. If she shows any indication of such conduct, she should be muzzled. Should she continue to attempt to bite for any length of time, it is generally because it is either too early or too late in the estrum cycle to consummate a breeding. If the bitch is small, sinks down when mounted, or won't stand, she must be held up. In some instances her owner or the stud's owner will have to kneel next to her, and with his hand under and between her hind legs, push the vulva up toward the dog's penis or guide the stud's penis into her vulva. Straw or earth, pushed under her hind legs to elevate her rear quarters, is effective in the case of a bitch who is very much too small for the stud.

As mentioned before, many novice bitch owners fail to recognize the initial signs of the oncoming heat period, or neglect to check, so that their knowledge of elapsed time since the first showing of red is only approximate. Many offer little aid in the attempt to complete the breeding, and talk incessantly and to no purpose, generally expressing wonder at their bitch's

At Cypress Kennels, Cypress, California, a stud
dog is introduced to a bitch in heat.

unorthodox conduct, but do little to quiet her. In many instances, particularly with a novice of the opposite sex, these actions are due to embarrassment. Regardless of the reason, remember to use the muzzle only on the bitch. We must always put the welfare of our dogs ahead of self.

MANAGING A STUD

There is not much more that can be written about the stud, except to caution the stud owner to be careful of using drugs or injections to make his dog eager to mate or more fertile. The number of puppies born in any litter is not dependent upon the healthy and fertile male's sperm, but upon the number of eggs the bitch gives off. Should your dog prove sterile, look for basic causes first. If there seems to be no physical reason for his sterility, then a series of injections by your veterinarian (perhaps of A-P-L, anterior-pituitary-like injections) might prove efficacious.

It is often a good idea to feed the dog a light meal before he is used, particularly if he is a reluctant stud. Young, or virgin, studs often regurgitate due to excitement, but it does them no harm. After the tie has broken, allow both dog and bitch to drink moderately.

How often a stud dog should be used is a moot question. The famous

A male and female Basset. Note how much bigger, heavier, and larger in head the male is.

Cocker Spaniel stud Red Brucie was bred to seven bitches the week before he died. I think we can truthfully say of this great dog that "he died happy." Consider also the fact that Brucie sired the famous "big four" litter when he was only about a year old.

Many other famous sires in other breeds have been, at the height of their popularity as studs, bred several times a week. It is the author's opinion that a strong, healthy Basset stud dog between the ages of three and eight years can be used 2 or 3 times a week with a week off every month.

I have known breeders, that small handful of the very lucky ones to have owned or bred a great stud dog, to have averaged over a long period of fertile years a very fine yearly income from the stud efforts of their animal.

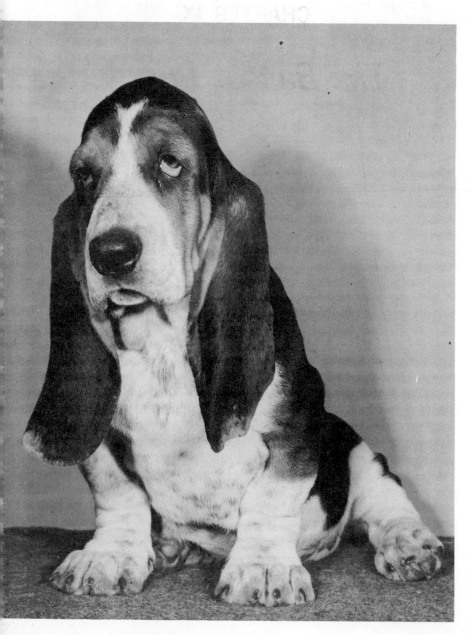

Ch. Santana-Mandeville's Agony by Ch. Huey of
Cypress x Ch. Beautiful Minnetonkie. Breeders,
owners, Santana-Mandeville Kennels.

CHAPTER IX

The Basset Puppy

The birth of a litter has been covered in a previous chapter on the brood bitch. As we indicated in that discussion, barring accident or complications at birth, there is little you can do for your puppies until they are approximately three weeks old. At that age supplementary feedings begin. But suppose that for one reason or another the mother must be taken from her brood: What care must be given to these small Bassets if they are to survive? Puppies need warmth. This is provided partly by their instinctive habit of gathering together in the nest, but to a much greater extent by the warmth of the mother's body. If the mother must be taken from the nest, this extra warmth can be provided by an ordinary light bulb, or, better still, an infra-red bulb, hung directly over the brood in the enclosed nest box.

CARE OF NEWBORNS

By far the most important requirement of these newborn pups is proper food. Puppies are belly and instinct, and nothing much more. They must be fed well and frequently. What shall we feed them, what formula can we arrive at that most closely approaches the natural milk of the mother, which we know is best? There are prepared modified milks for orphan puppies which are commercially available and very worth while, or you can mix your own formula of ingredients which will most closely simulate natural bitch's milk. To do this, you must first know the basic quality of the dam's milk. Bitches' milk is comparatively acid; it contains less sugar and water, more ash and protein, and far more fat than cow or human milk, so we must modify our formula to conform to these differences.

To begin, purchase a can of Nestlés Pelargon, a spray-dried, acidified, and homogenized modified milk product. If you can't get Pelargon, try any of the spray-dried baby milks, but Pelargon is best since it is, like bitches' milk, slightly acid and rich in necessary nutritive substances. To one ounce of the modified milk product, add one ounce of fresh cream. Pour six ounces of water by volume into this mixture and blend with an electric mixer or egg beater until it is smooth. Larger amounts can be mixed employing the same basic proportions and kept refrigerated. This formula should be fed five or six times a day and, when fed, must be warmed to body heat. Many puppies refuse to drink a formula which has not been warmed to just the right temperature.* Do not add lime water, glucose, or dextrose to the formula, for by so doing you are modifying in the wrong direction. An ordinary baby's bottle and nipple are adequate as the formula vehicle. Never drop liquids directly in the puppy's throat with an eye dropper or you invite pneumonia. A twelve ounce puppy will absorb one ounce of formula at each feeding. A valuable adjunct to the puppy's diet, whether formula or breast fed, is two drops of Dietol, dropped into the lip pocket from the first day of birth on, the amount to be increased with greater growth and age. A bottle trough can be built for orphan pups. The trick here is to space the nipple holes so that the bodies of the pups touch when drinking.

If it is possible to find a foster mother for orphan pups, your troubles are over. Most lactating bitches will readily take to puppies other than their own if the new babies are first prepared by spreading some of the foster mother's milk over their tiny bodies. The foster mother will lick them clean and welcome them to the nest. Dewclaws should be clipped off with a manicure scissors the day after birth.

WEANING

When the puppies are two-and-a-half to three weeks old the dam will often engage in an action that is disgusting to the neophyte, but which is an instinctive and natural performance to the bitch. She will regurgitate her own stomach contents of partially digested food for her puppies to eat, thus beginning, in her own way, the weaning process. If you have begun supplementary feeding in time, this action by the bitch will seldom occur. If you haven't, it is a definite indication that supplementary feeding should begin at once.

Puppies grow best on milk, meat, fat, and cereal diets. Growth is attained through proteins, but proteins differ, so that puppies fed on vegetable protein diets will not grow and thrive as well as those fed animal proteins. Vitamins E and K (found in alfalfa meal) are essential to the pups' well being and should be used in adequate amounts in the food ration. Remember that 70 per cent of the pup's energy is derived from fat intake, so supply this food element generously in the diet. Lime water should not be incorporated in the diet since it neutralizes stomach acidity, a condition which is necessary to the assimilation of fat. In experiments, puppies on fat-free diets developed deficiency symptoms charac-

* Warm goat's milk is also excellent for Basset puppies.

110

A closeup of newly born Basset puppies.

terized by anemia, weight loss, dull coats, and finally, death. Fat alone could not cure the advanced manifestation of the condition, indicating that some metabolic process was disturbed when complete fat removal in the diet was resorted to. But feeding butterfat plus folacin resulted in dramatic cures.

To begin the small puppy on supplementary feeding, place the pan of food before him, gently grasp his head behind the ears, and dip his lips and chin into the food. The puppy will lick his lips, taste the food, and in no time at all learn to feed by himself. Be careful not to push the head in so far that the pup's nose is covered and clogged by food.

Check the puppies' navels every day to see that infection has not set in. This infection comes from the scraping of their soft bellies on a rough surface and can generally be avoided if several thicknesses of cloth covers the floor of the nest box under the bedding.

Clip the sharp little nails to avoid damage to litter mates' eyes, which will open at about ten days. Have a fecal check made when the pups are about three-and-a-half weeks old. If they are infested with worms, worm

Three gorgeous puppies from Dr. Skolnick''s
Slippery Hill Kennels, representing the Hound
colors: tricolor, tan and red.

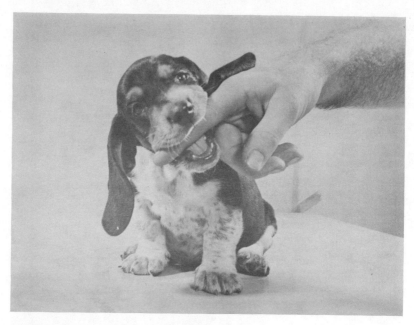

Pups like this seven-week-old Basset should be
given toys to cut their teeth on, not fingers.

them immediately. Do not attempt to build up the pups first if the parasitic infestation has made them unthrifty. It is best to rid them of the
worms quickly, after which they will speedily return to normal health
and plumpness.

The weeks fly by, and before you know it the puppies are at saleable
age. The breeder, you can be sure, has not wasted these weeks. He has
spent many hours in close observation of the litter and has centered his
interest on one pup which he thinks shows the most promise. Either he
will hold this pup for himself, sell him to a show-conscious buyer, or
keep the puppy and sell it at a higher price when it has become more
fully developed and its early promise becomes a fact. The strange part
about this whole business of picking a young puppy from a litter is that
the novice buyer many times stands as good a chance of picking the best
pup as the seasoned and experienced breeder. The reason for this seem-
ing incongruity lies in the fact that in every litter there will be several
pups which, if well bred and well cared for, appear to be potential winners
at eight to ten weeks of age. Another reason concerns the ratio of sectional
growth in young animals. Each pup, as an individual, will have a different growth rate and exhibit change in relative sections of the body, as
well as in over-all growth, from day to day.

114

BUYING A PUPPY

If you are the potential purchaser of a Basset puppy, or a grown dog for that matter, prepare yourself for the purchase first by attending as many shows as possible, especially shows where known Basset Hound authorities are officiating. Observe, absorb, and listen. Visit kennels which have well-bred, winning stock, and at shows and kennels make an unholy nuisance of yourself by asking innumerable questions of people who have proved, by their record in the breed, that information gleaned from them can be respected. When you intend to purchase a new car, or an electrical appliance such as a refrigerator or washing machine, you go to sales rooms and examine the different makes, weighing their features and quality, one against the other. You inquire of friends who have different brands their opinion in regard to the utility value of the item, and, when you have made up your mind which brand is best, you make sure that you purchase the item from a reliable distributor. Do the same thing when you intend to purchase a dog. Before you make your journey to any breeder to buy a puppy, be sure to inquire first into the background of the breeder as well as the background of his dogs. What does this breeder actually know about his breed? What has he formerly produced? What is his reputation amongst other reputable breeders? Does his stock have balanced minds as well as balanced bodies? Find the answers to these questions even before you delve into the ancestry of the puppies he has for sale. If the answers prove that this breeder is an honest, dependable person with more than a smattering knowledge of the breed, and that he has bred consistently typical stock, then your next step will be to study the breeding of his puppies to determine whether they have been bred from worth-while stock which comes from good producing strains. Examine stock he has sold from different breedings to other customers. Be careful of kennels which are puppy factories, breeding solely for commercial reasons, and don't be carried away by hysterical, overdone, adjective-happy advertisements.

When you have satisfied yourself that the breeder is a morally responsible person who has good stock, then you may sally forth to purchase your future champion. It is best, if possible, to invite an experienced breeder to accompany you on your mission. As mentioned before, even the most experienced cannot with assurance pick the pup in the litter which will mature into the best specimen. An experienced person can, however, keep you from selecting a very engaging youngster which exhibits obvious faults which quite possibly won't improve.

Assuming that the litter from which you are going to select your puppy is a fat and healthy one and it is a male puppy you have set your heart on having, ask the breeder to separate the sexes so you can examine the male pups only. Normal puppies are friendly, lovable creatures wanting immediate attention, so the little fellow who backs away from you and runs away and hides should be eliminated from consideration immediately. This also applies to the pup which sulks in a corner and wants no part of the proceedings. Watch the puppies from a distance of approximately twenty feet as they play and frolic, sometimes trotting and occasionally quitting their play for a fleeting moment to stand gazing at something of interest which has, for that second, engaged their attention. Don't be rushed. Take all the time necessary to pick the puppy you want. You are about to pay cold cash for a companion who will be with you for many years.

If you have been lucky enough to have had the opportunity of examining both sire and dam (or hunted behind them), determine which puppies exhibit the faults of the parents or the strain. If any particular fault seems to be overdone in a specific pup, discard him from further consideration. Do not handle the pups during this preliminary examination. Look for over-all balance first and the absence of glaring structural faults, but remember that the good pup will show an exaggeration of all the excellencies you expect to be present in the mature animal.

The feet of the good Basset puppy should be large and the pup should give the overall appearance of having very heavy bone. He should be long and low with a graceful dip downward through the chest area but not too much tuck-up in the belly. Even though his legs are short and he has the ungainliness of his youth he should track true, fore and aft. Make sure his hindquarters are full and thick through the thigh and he moves true going away from you. You want no indication of lack of balance or coordination here. In profile the puppy should show a nice flare in stifle. This will straighten a bit as he matures so a bit of exaggeration when young is necessary here.

Examine the pup's mouth; see that his bite is the correct scissors bite. He should have dark, soulful eyes and his ears should be set on very low and be exceedingly long and the "leather" thin. We want no roach in the back, even in the young pup. Neither do we want a definite dip or "sway" in the back. This latter fault gets worse with age and becomes particu-larly pronounced in bitches after a litter.

The frontal bone (cartilage really) or prosternum juts well forward and ahead of the shoulders forming a "prow." The rib cage should be smooth and long and extend well back so that even though the Basset's body is long the loin is not too long. The shoulders must be well laid back and the skin very loose and supple all over the body and especially on the head where it can be pushed forward into deep folds. The puppy's

A female and a male puppy, both three months of age. Note the comparative refinements of the bitch pup. Below is a puppy snapshot of Ch. Slippery Hill Oliver Onion, displaying exceptional ear length and quality.

At Slippery Hill Kennels; teaching a lovely open marked puppy to assume a show pose. Below, at the same kennels, we see a large tub filled with quality two-month-old youngsters.

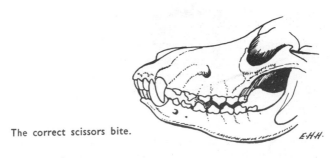

The correct scissors bite.

E·H·H·

feet must be nicely knuckled up, never splayed, thin or weak. The tail, or stern, should be carried out and up like a sabre, well haired, stout and strong. All in all, the Basset puppy should possess a "breedy" look, hard to define but recognized when present.

For a gun or field dog, select an animal that is well up to size with good legs and feet, thick tough footpads, deep in the jaw, strong all over and showing exceptional willingness, intelligence and staunchness to sound. An open, hound marked dog is more easily seen in the field than an almost solid colored specimen.

In each instance, whether for show or field, select a puppy whose ancestry indicates that he was bred for your purpose.

If you desire only a pet, look for intelligence, willingness, sweetness, good health and generally good Basset type, color being of no importance.

Female puppies are generally slightly smaller and show a greater degree of refinement than the males.

Remember that no one can pick a champion at eight weeks and no breeder can truthfully sell you a future winner at that age. All a breeder can guarantee is the health and breeding of the puppy, and the fact that he possesses the normal complement of eyes, ears and legs. The best you can do if you are observant, knowing, and lucky, is to pick the best pup in that particular litter, at that particular time.

THE PUPPY IN A NEW HOME

If it is at all possible, it is best to purchase two pups at the same time. They furnish company for each other, eliminate lonesome serenades during the first few nights, and are competition at the food pan. If you bring home only one pup, provide him with a stuffed dog or doll in his sleeping box which you have taken to the breeder's with you and rubbed in the nest box. This will frequently give the puppy some sense of comfort and companionship and alleviate lonesomeness that brings on dismal howling during the first night in his new home. A ticking alarm clock near the pup's bed will sometimes have the same effect.

In his new home, amidst strange surroundings, the pup will very often go off his feed for a time. This should not unduly alarm you unless his refusal to eat lasts so long that he becomes emaciated. If this occurs, ask your veterinarian for a good tonic, or change diets to tempt his palate. Never coax him or resort to forced feeding, or you will immediately spoil your pup and be a slave to him and his aggravating eating habits from that time forward. If he eats only one or two meals a day, instead of the several feedings he should have, he will survive until his appetite improves if he is otherwise healthy and vigorous. Should you find after a reasonable time and much scheming and effort that you have a naturally finicky eater, you must resign yourself to the fact that you have acquired a headache which can last for the duration of your dog's life and one which cannot be cured by aspirin. Only heroic measures can help you conquer this difficulty, and you must steel yourself and cast out pity if you are to succeed. He must be starved, but really starved, until he has reached a point where dry bread resembles the most succulent beef. Only by such drastic measures can a finicky eater be cured. Dogs who have the competition of other dogs, or even a cat, at the feed pan usually display a normal appetite. For this reason it is sometimes smart for the one-dog owner to borrow a freind's or neighbor's pet to feed with his

Arriving in a new home, this Basset puppy has
been supplied with his own private bed. He will
also need love to make him forget his litter mates.

120

Children and Bassets make a wonderful team, but the pup must be given plenty of time to sleep.

own until such time as his own dog has acquired a healthful and adequate appetite.

Be careful when handling your Basset pup. His huge bones are easily bruised and his weight, compared to his body length, makes him ungainly. When you pick him up make sure you balance him evenly in your arms with one hand under his hindquarters. Don't allow him to jump or run up and down steep stairs until he becomes older, his bones have set, and he is more capable of balancing his weight, bulk and peculiar physical build with ease and assurance.

Arrange for your pup to have lots of sleep, particularly after feeding, a difficult chore when there are youngsters in the home, but nevertheless very necessary to the well being of the pup. Make him feel at home so he will respond quickly to his new surroundings. It so often happens that a puppy retained by the breeder surpasses at maturity the purchased pup who was a better specimen in the beginning. This confounds the novice, yet has a reasonably simple explanation. The retained pup had no change in environment which would affect his appetite and well being during the critical period of growth, while the bought pup had and so was outstripped by his lesser litter brother.

Your puppy will have two sets of teeth, the milk teeth, which will

A chairful of pups bred by Edward J. Ellis of Clearwater, Florida.

The same Ellis puppies getting some sun. They are by Simono El Mil x Priscilla Bone-a-Part.

have fallen out by the time he is approximately six months of age, and the permanent teeth, which he'll retain for the rest of his life. Loss of weight and fever may accompany the eruption of the new, permanent teeth, but is no cause for alarm. Anatomists have a simple formula to represent the number and arrangement of permanent teeth which, at a glance, will allow you to determine if your dog has his full complement of teeth, and if he hasn't, which ones are missing. In the chart below, the horizontal line represents the division between upper and lower jaw. We begin with the incisors in the front of the dog's mouth and designate them with the letter I. The canine teeth are labeled C, the premolars, P, and the molars, M. The complete formula for a dog possessing all his teeth would be:

$$I \frac{3+3}{3+3} + C \frac{1+1}{1+1} + P \frac{4+4}{4+4} + M \frac{2+2}{3+3} = 42 \text{ teeth} \quad \begin{array}{l} \text{(20 in upper jaw)} \\ \text{(22 in lower jaw)} \end{array}$$

Showing the length to which some ears will go to
get attention. No, the pup's name is not Dumbo.

Barney, a nice three-month-old male puppy.
Below, a youngster being groomed. Begin
brushing early so the pup will get used to it.

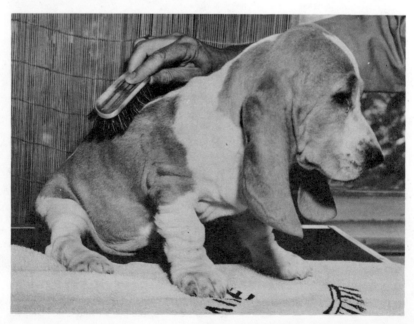

Occasionally, puppies develop lip warts which will disappear in a short time, leaving no after effects. Remember to have your puppy immunized against distemper and hepatitis and, as much as possible, keep him away from other dogs until he is old enough to combat the diseases which take their toll of the very young. Lastly, but of great importance, give your pup the opportunity to develop that character and charm for which the Basset Hound is justly famed. Give him human companionship and understanding, take him with you in the car and amongst strangers. Let him live the normal, happy, and useful life which is his heritage, and that tiny bundle of fur which you brought home so short a time ago will grow into a canine citizen of whom you will be proud to say, "He's mine."

Ch. Santana-Mandeville Just Fred.

CHAPTER X

Fundamental Obedience Training

Responsibility for the reputation of any breed is shared by everyone who owns a specimen of that breed. Reputation, good or bad, is achieved by conduct, and conduct is the result of the molding, through training, of inherent character into specific channels of behavior.

It is a distinct pleasure, to novice, old-timer, or the public at large, to watch dogs perform which have been trained to special tasks. Here is the ultimate, the end result of the relationship between man and dog. After watching an inspired demonstration, we sometimes wonder if, under a proper training regime, our own dog could do as well. Perhaps he can if he is temperamentally fitted for the task we have in mind. No single individual of any breed, regardless of breed type, temperament, and inheritance, is fitted to cope with all the branches of specialized service. Nor does every owner possess the qualifications or experience necessary to train dogs successfully to arduous tasks. But every dog can be trained in the fundamentals of decent behavior, and every dog owner can give his dog this basic training. It is, indeed, the duty of every dog owner to teach his dog obedience to command as well as the necessary fundamentals of training which insure good conduct and gentlemanly deportment. A dog that is uncontrolled can become a nuisance and even a menace. This dog brings grief to his owner and bad reputation to himself and the breed he represents.

We cannot attempt, in this limited space, to write a complete and comprehensive treatise on all the aspects of dog training. There are several worthwhile books, written by experienced trainers, that cover the entire varied field of initial and advanced training. There are, furthermore, hundreds of training classes throughout the country where both the dog and its owner receive standard obedience training for a nominal fee, under the guidance of experienced trainers. Here in these pages you will find only specific suggestions on some points of simple basic training which we feel are neglected in most of the books on this subject. We will also attempt to give you basic reasons for training techniques and explain natural limitations to aid you in eliminating future, perhaps drastic, mistakes.

The key to all canine training, simple or advanced, is control. Once you have established control over your Basset, you can, if you so desire, progress to advanced or specialized training. The dog's only boundaries to learning are his own basic limitations. This vital control must be established during the basic training in good manners.

Almost every Basset is responsive to training. He loves his master and finds delight in pleasing him. To approach the training problem with your Basset, to make it a pleasant and easy intimacy rather than an arduous and wearisome task, you must first learn a few fundamentals. In the preceding paragraph we spoke of control as the paramount essential in training. To gain control over your dog, you must first establish control over your own vagaries of temperament. During training, when you lose your temper, you lose control. Shouting, nagging repetition, angry reprimand, and exasperation only confuse your canine pupil. If he does not obey, then the lesson has not been learned. He needs teaching, not punishment. The time of training should be approached with pleasure by both master and dog, so that both you and your pupil look forward to these periods of contact. If you establish this atmosphere, your dog will enjoy working, and a dog who enjoys his work, who is constantly trying to please, is a dog who is always under control.

Consistency is the brother of control in training. Perform each movement used in schooling in the same manner every time. Use the same words of command or communication without variance. Employ command words that are simple, single syllables, chosen for their crispness and difference in sound. Don't call your dog to you one day with the command, "Come," and the next day, with the command, "Here," and expect the animal to understand and perform the act with alacrity. Inconsistency confuses your dog. If you are inconsistent, the dog will not perform correctly and your control is lost. By consistency you establish habit patterns which eventually become an inherent part of your Basset's behavior. Remember that a few simple commands, well learned, are much better than many and varied commands only partially absorbed. Therefore be certain that your dog completely understands a command and will perform the action it demands, quickly and without hesitation, before attempting to teach him a new command.

Before we begin training, we must first assess our prospective pupil's intelligence and character. We must understand that his eyesight is not as keen as ours, but that he is quick to notice movement. We must know that sound and scent are his chief means of communication with his world, and that in these departments he is far superior to us. We must

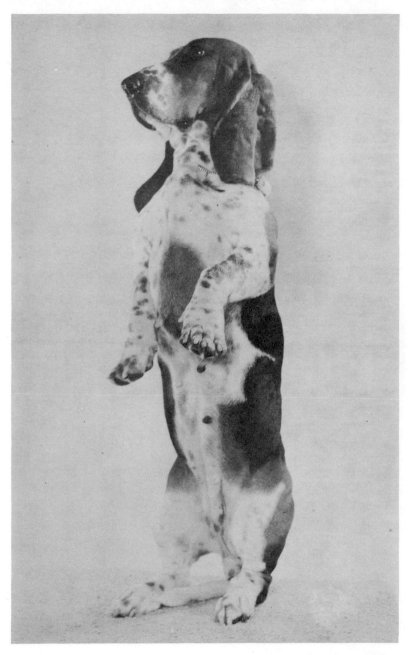

The famous television star Cleo is an example of
how far training can go with a Basset.

"No" is one of the most important words in the
training vocabulary. The gesture helps, too.

reach him, then, through voice and gesture, and realize that he is very sensitive to quality change and intonation of the commanding voice. Therefore, any given command must have a definite tonal value in keeping with its purpose. The word "No" used in reprimand must be expressed sharply and with overtones of displeasure, while "Good boy," employed as praise, should be spoken lightly and pleasantly. In early training, the puppy recognizes distinctive sound coupled with the quality of tone used rather than individual words. *

All words of positive command should be spoken sharply and distinctly during training. By this we do not mean that commands must be shouted, a practice which seems to be gaining favor in obedience work and which is very much to be deplored. A well-trained, mature Basset can be kept completely under control and will obey quickly and willingly when commands are given in an ordinary conversational tone. The first word a puppy learns is the word-sound of his name; therefore, in training, his name should be spoken first to attract his attention to the command which follows. Thus, when we want our dog to come to us, and his name is Pierre, we command, "Pierre! Come!"

Intelligence varies in dogs as it does in all animals, human or otherwise. The ability to learn and to perform is limited by intelligence, facets of character, and structure, such as willingness, energy, sensitivity, aggressiveness, stability, and functional ability. The sensitive dog must be handled with greater care and quietness in training than the less sensitive animal. Aggressive dogs must be trained with firmness, and an animal which possesses a structural fault which makes certain of the physical aspects of training a painful experience cannot be expected to perform these acts with enjoyment and consistency.

In referring to intelligence, we mean, of course, canine intelligence. Dogs are supposedly unable to reason, since that portion of the brain which, in humans, is the seat of the reasoning power is not highly developed in the dog. Yet there have been so many reported incidents of canine behavior that seemingly could not have been actuated by instinct, training, stored knowledge, or the survival factor that we are led to wonder if the dog may not possess some primitive capacity for reasoning which, in essence, is so different from the process of human reasoning that it has been overlooked, or is as yet beyond the scope of human comprehension.

Training begins the instant the puppies in the nest feel the touch of your hand and are able to hear the sound of your voice. Once the pup is old enough to run and play, handle him frequently, petting him, making a fuss over him, speaking in soothing and pleasant tones and repeating his

---

* For more detailed information on basic training see the author's book, How To Train Your Dog, published by TFH Publications, Inc.

The "No" command is used to train your Basset
to stay off furniture. Below is illustrated a first
step in paper-breaking the puppy.

name over and over again. When you bring him his meals, call him by name and coax him to "Come." As time passes, he associates the command "Come" with a pleasurable experience and will come immediately upon command. Every time he obeys a command, he should be praised or rewarded. When calling your puppies to their food, it is good practice to use some kind of distinguishing sound accompanying the command— a clucking or "beep" sound. It is amazing how this distinctive sound will be retained by the dog's memory, so that years after it has ceased to be used, he will still remember and respond to the sound.

LEAD TRAINING

Some professional trainers and handlers put soft collars on tiny pups, with a few inches of thin rope attached to the collar clip. The puppies, in play, tug upon these dangling pieces of rope hanging from the collars of their litter mates, thus preparing the youngsters for easy leash breaking in the future. In training the pup to the leash, be sure to use a long leash, and coax, do not drag the reluctant puppy, keeping him always on your left side. Never use the leash as an implement of punishment.

HOUSEBREAKING

Housebreaking is usually the tragedy of the novice dog owner. We who have Bassets are fortunate in this respect since, as a breed, they are basically clean in habits and quite easily housebroken. Many Bassets which are raised outside in a run never need to be actually housebroken, preferring to use the ground for their act and seemingly sensing the fact that the house is not to be soiled. Dogs tend to defecate in areas which they, or other dogs, have previously soiled, and will go to these spots if given the chance. Directly after eating or waking a puppy almost inevitably has to relieve himself. If he is in the house and makes a mistake, it is generally your fault, as you should have recognized these facts and removed him in time to avert disaster. If, after you have taken him out, he comes in and soils the floor or rug, he must be made to realize that he has done wrong. Scold him with, "Shame! Shame!" and rush him outside. Praise him extravagantly when he has taken advantage of the great outdoors. Sometimes if you catch him preparing to void in the house, a quick, sharp, "No" will stop the proceedings and allow you time to usher him out. Never rub his nose in his excreta. Never indulge in the common practice of striking the puppy with a rolled up newspaper or with your hand. If you do, you may be training your dog either to be hand shy, to be shy of paper, or to bite the newsboy. Your hand should be used only in such a way that your dog recognizes it as that part of you which implements your voice, to pet and give pleasure. In housebreaking, a "No," or "Shame" appropriately used and delivered in an admonishing tone is punishment enough.

A working Basset is seldom broken to paper in the house. If your dog has been so trained and subsequently you wish to train him to use the outdoors, a simple way to teach him this is to move the paper he has used outside, anchoring it with stones. Lead the dog to the paper when you know he is ready to void. Each day make the paper smaller until it has completely disappeared, and the pup will have formed the habit of going on the spot previously occupied by the paper. Puppies tend to prefer to void on a surface similar in texture to that which they used in their first few weeks of life. Thus a pup who has had access to an outside run is easily housebroken, preferring the feel of ground under him.

If your Basset is to be a housedog, a lot of grief can be avoided by remembering a few simple rules. Until he is thoroughly clean in the house, confine him to one room at night, preferably a tile or linoleum-floored room that can be cleaned easily. Tie him so that he cannot get beyond the radius of his bed, or confine him to a dog house within the room; few dogs will soil their beds or sleeping quarters. Feed at regular hours and you will soon learn the interval between the meal and its natural result and take the pup out in time. Give water only after meals until he is housebroken. Puppies, like inveterate drunks, will drink constantly if the means is available, and there is no other place for surplus water to go but out. The result is odd puddles at odd times.

TRAINING FOR GOOD MANNERS

"No," "Shame," "Come," and "Good boy" (or "girl"), spoken in appropriate tones, are the basic communications you will use in initial training.

If your pup is running free and he doesn't heed your command to come, do not chase him—he will only run away or dodge your attempts to catch him and your control over him will be completely lost. Attract his attention by calling his name, and when he looks in your direction, turn and run away from him, calling him as you do so. In most instances he will quickly run after you. Even if it takes a great deal of time and much exasperation to get him to come to you, never scold him once he has. Praise him instead. *A puppy should only be scolded when he is caught in the act of doing something he shouldn't do.* If he is scolded even a few minutes after he has committed his error, he will not associate the punishment with the crime and

Bassets are good "Obedience" dogs. The top
illustration shows a Basset being trained to
"Heel." Below, a Basset is being taught to "Sit."
Pull up on the lead and push down on the dog's
croup, forcing him into the "Sit" position.
Use his name followed by
the command, "Sit."

When teaching your dog to "Come," use the
long lead, a vocal command, and gently pull him
toward you. The "Stay" command is initially
taught from the "Sit" position, as shown below.

The Basset has been taught to "Come" and sits
correctly in front of his trainer. Below, Joie's
Buttons of Beau, C.D.X. executes the correct
"Come" while retrieving a dumbbell.

will be bewildered and unhappy about the whole thing, losing his trust in you.

Puppies are inveterate thieves. It is natural for them to steal food from the table. The "No!" and "Shame!" command, or reprimands, should be used to correct this breach of manners. The same commands are employed when the pup uses your living room couch as a sleeping place. Many times dogs are aware that they must not sleep on the furniture, but are clever enough to avoid punishment by using the sofa only when you are out. They will hastily leave the soft comfort of the couch when they hear you approaching and greet you in wide-eyed innocence, models of canine virtue. Only the tell-tale hairs, the dent in the cushion, and the body heat on the fabric are clues to the culprit's dishonesty. This recalls the tale of the dog who went just a step further. So clever was he that when his master approached, he would leap from the couch and, standing before it, blow upon the cushions to dislodge the loose hairs and cool the cushion's surface. The hero of this tale of canine duplicity was not identified as to breed, but we are sure that such intelligence could only have been displayed by a Basset.

If, like the dog in the story, the pup persists in committing this mis-

A Basset Hound working in advanced Obedience classes takes the high jump carrying a dumbbell which he has retrieved and will bring back to his trainer.

Another Basset also working in advanced
Obedience is taken over the broad jump by his
trainer.

demeanor, we must resort to another method to cure him. Where before we used a positive approach, we must now employ a negative, and rather sneaky method. The idea is to trick the pup into thinking that when he commits these crimes he punishes himself and that we have been attempting to stop him from bringing this punishment down upon his head. To accomplish this end with the unregenerate food thief, tie a tempting morsel of food to a long piece of string. To the string attach several empty tin cans, or small bells, eight to ten inches apart. Set the whole contraption on the kitchen or dining-room table, with the food morsel perched temptingly on an accessible edge. Leave the room and allow the little thief to commit his act of dishonesty. When you hear the resultant racket, rush into the room, sternly mouthing the appropriate words of reproach. You will generally find a thoroughly chastened pup who, after one or two such lessons, will eye any tabled food askance and leave it strictly alone.

The use of mousetraps is a neat little trick to cure the persistent sofa-hopper. Place two or three set traps on the couch area the dog prefers and cover them with a sheet of newspaper. When he jumps on up the sofa, he will spring the traps and leave that vicinity in a great and startled hurry.

These methods, or slight variations, can be used in teaching your pup

In advanced Obedience a Basset is given a hand
scent before sending him to find an article
handled by the trainer (scent discrimination).

to resist many youthful temptations such as dragging and biting rugs, furniture, tablecloths, draperies, curtains, etc.

The same approach, in essence, is useful in teaching the pup not to jump up on your friends and neighbors. You can lose innumerable friends if your mud-footed dog playfully jumps up on the visitor wearing a new suit or dress. If the "No" command alone does not break him of this habit, hold his front legs and feet tightly in your hands when he jumps up, and retain your hold. The pup finds himself in an uncomfortable and unnatural position standing on his hind legs alone. He will soon tug and pull to release his front legs from your hold. Retain your hold in the face of his struggles until he is heartily sick of the strained position he is in. A few such lessons and he will refrain from committing an act which brings such discomfort in its wake.

Remember that only by positive training methods can you gain control which is the basis of successful training, and these tricky methods do not give you that control. They are simply short-cut ways of quickly rectifying nuisance habits, but do nothing to establish the "rapport" which must exist between trainer and dog.

During the entire puppy period the basis is being laid for other and more advanced training. The acts of discipline, of everyday handling,

Pierre's Bonne Soie, U.D., finds and retrieves the proper article. The Basset's fantastic scenting ability aids in this exercise.

grooming, and feeding, are preparation for the time when he is old enough to be taught the meaning of the Sit, Down, Heel, Stand, and Stay, commands which are the first steps in obedience training and commands which every dog should be taught to obey immediately. Once you have learned how to train your dog and have established complete control, further training is only limited by your own abilities and by the natural boundaries which exist within the animal himself.

Don't rush your training. Be patient with small progress. Training for both you and your dog will become easier as you progress. Make sure that whatever you teach him is well and thoroughly learned, and it will never be forgotten. Remember to use simple common sense when you approach the task of training. Approach it with ease and confidence. Control yourself if you wish to control your dog, for control is the vital element in all training. Realize the limitations as well as the abilities of your dog, and the final product of your training zeal will bring you pride in accomplishment, pride in yourself and your ability, and pride in your Basset.

Ch. Slippery Hill Paprika winning Best of
Breed at the Tidewater Kennel Club, 1969.
From Slippery Hill Bassets.

CHAPTER XI

Training for the Show Ring

So many things of beauty or near perfection are so often marred and flawed by an improper approach to their finish. A Renoir or an El Greco tacked frameless to a bathroom wall is no less a thing of art, yet loses importance by its limited environment and presentation. Living things, too, need this finish and preparation to exhibit their worth to full advantage. The beauty of a flower goes unrecognized if withered petals and leaves mar its perfection, and the living wonder of a fine dog is realized only in those moments when he stands or moves in quiet and balanced beauty. The show ring is a ready frame in which to display your dog. The manner in which he is presented within that frame is up to you.

If you contemplate showing your Basset, as so many of you who read this book do, it is of the utmost importance that your dog be as well and fully trained for exhibition as he is for general gentlemanly conduct in the home. Insufficient or improper training, or faulty handling, can result in lower show placings than your dog deserves and can quite conceivably ruin an otherwise promising show career. In the wider sense, and of even more importance to the breed as a whole, is the impression your Basset in the show ring projects to the gallery. Every Basset shown becomes a representative of the breed in the eyes of the onlookers, so that each dog becomes a symbol of all Basset Hounds when he is on exhibition. Inside the ring ropes, your dog will be evaluated by the judges as an individual; beyond the ropes, a breed will be judged by the behavior of your dog.

When you enter your Basset in a show, you do so because you believe that he or she is a good enough specimen of the breed to afford competition to, and perhaps win over, the other dogs entered. If your dog is as good as you think he is, he certainly deserves to be shown to full advantage if you expect him to win or place in this highly competitive sport. A novice handler with a quality Basset which is untrained, unruly, or phlegmatic cannot give competition to a dog of equal, or even lesser, merit which is well trained and handled to full advantage.

Novice owners frequently bring untrained dogs to shows so that they can become accustomed to the strange proceedings and surroundings,

143

Slippery Hill Reba going Best of Winners at the
Maryland Basset Hound Specialty. Breeder,
owner, handler, Dr. Skolnick. Note regal head
carriage and strong topline. Quality and elegance.

144

hopefully thinking that, in time, the dog will learn to behave in the wanted manner by himself. Often the novice's training for the show ring begins in desperate and intense endeavor within the show ring itself. Confusion for both dog and handler can be the only result of such a program. Preparation for showing must begin long in advance of actual show competition for both dog and handler.

ADVANCE PREPARATION

Let us assume that you have been fortunate enough to breed or purchase a puppy who appears to possess all the necessary qualifications for a successful show career. Training for that career should begin from the moment you bring him home, or if you are the breeder, from the time he is weaned. This early training essentially follows the same pattern as does fundamental training in conduct. Again you begin by establishing between you and the puppy the happy relationship which, in time, becomes the control so necessary to all training. Handle the puppy frequently, brush him, examine his teeth, set him up in a show stance, and stroke his back slowly. Move him on a loose leash, talking to him constantly in a happy, friendly tone. Make all your movements in a deliberate and quiet manner. Praise and pat the puppy often, establishing an easy and happy rapport during this period. This is simple early preparation for the more exact training to come.

During this period the owner and prospective handler should take the opportunity to refresh or broaden his own knowledge. Reread the standard, and with this word picture in mind, build a mental reproduction of the perfect Basset: his structure, balance, gait, and movement. Critically observe the better handlers at shows to see how they set and gait their dogs. Only by accumulating insight and knowledge such as this can you succeed in the training which will bring out the best features of your own future show dog.

SHOW GROOMING

It is time now to learn something of the art of show grooming or preparing, known to the professional as "putting down." For the novice it may be the better part of valor to allow a professional handler to do the initial job, observing the preparation closely and asking many "why" questions. The idea of the show preparation is to trim your dog to look his best, to follow the standard for the breed as closely as possible, and to hide faults and bring out virtues with your handling. The latter cannot be considered "faking." You are merely attempting to make your dog

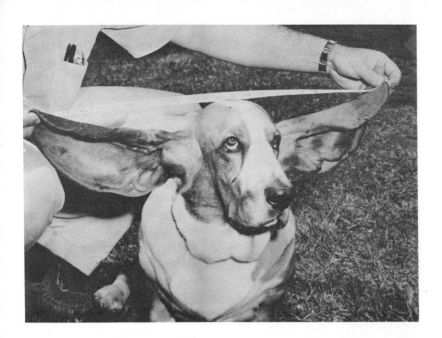

Great length of ear is one of the necessary
features of showing and breeding Basset Hound.

look as perfect as possible, and it is up to the judge to find the disguised faults.

Show preparation is fairly simple for a Basset. Essentially you must have your dog up to weight and in excellent health and good coat. Clean the eyes, ears and teeth and clip the toenails short. Muscle tone in a short coated hound is important. Your Basset must look as though he could go out in the field and hunt all day.

With a barber's shears trim all excess hair from the face, particularly the long muzzle hairs and the eyebrows and cheek hairs. Trim uneven hairs from the underbody-line and those around the feet and in back of the legs. Cut back a bit on the ragged hair at the base of the tail. With a little practice this can all be done without leaving telltale scissors marks.

White chalk rubbed into white sections of the coat and then thoroughly brushed out will make these parts whiter than white, and a bit of coat dressing rubbed into the palms and then over the dark areas of your dog's coat will give it a nice finish.

RING MANNERS

Now that our young show ring aspirant is trimmed and beautified, let us train him in show-ring deportment. The early training you have given him as a very young puppy to stand for handling is the basis from which you must work. Make him stand at your command. If his front legs aren't exactly right correct his stance by putting your hand under his chest directly behind the front legs, lifting and gently setting him down again into the right forehand position, with his legs parallel. Next put your hand between his hind legs and raise him and set him down so that his hindquarters slope back showing a good bend of stifle and with the hocks exactly perpendicular to the floor. Viewed from behind the legs should be straight. The position of the hind legs should also shape the back to a straight line to the tail.

Now raise your dog's head and the leash high. But be careful that you don't pull the ears up with the leash and make them appear higher set than they are. Make him also pose perfectly without the leash.

Teach him to hold this pose for ever longer periods of time with the

. One way to get correct front alignment when teaching dog to pose is to lift the front end and then gently drop it for a natural show stance.

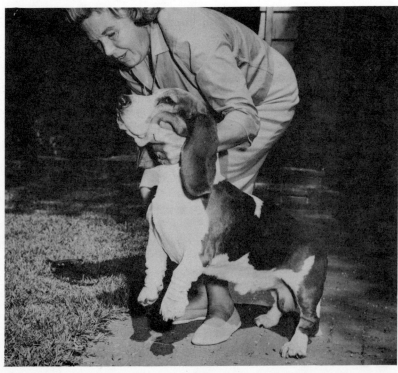

Speak to your Basset quietly, making him hold
the front stance while you gently hand-set his
hindquarters into the correct show position.

reward of a tiny piece of some kind of tidbit. All the movements you make
around the dog when setting him up, etc., must be done slowly and gently.
Never grab him by the tail to pick up his hindquarters; he will resent it and
inevitably squat. Be patient and watch the better professional handlers
and you will soon have your Basset standing like a show ring veteran.

When you move your dog listen to the judge's directions when you are
in the ring. When you are training your Basset make him move straight
and with small jerks of the lead make him keep his head up. The Basset
has a tendency to drop his nose to the ground when moving. Use the
leash held straight and up away from your body so that it forms a fairly
taut line, to foil his natural instincts and oblige him to keep his head
raised as he moves trappily along. Once he has learned this lesson he
should be taught to move on a loose leash with his head up, to swing along
proudly and naturally. His gait and natural balance will be better than if
he is "hung" up by a tight lead while moving, a practice much in vogue
with certain handlers.

When you come to the end of the allotted run and turn to start back,
do not jerk the dog around; instead give him more leash freedom and
allow him to come around easily without a change of hands, meanwhile

speaking to him quietly. When he has completed the turn, draw him to you with the leash and continue moving back to the starting point. At the finish, pat and praise him.

While you are teaching your dog the elements of ring deportment, take stock of the pupil himself. To do this correctly, you will need assistance. Have someone else put the dog through his paces, handling him as you have and as he will be handled in the show ring. Observe the dog carefully to determine when he looks his best. Should he be stretched out a bit when posing? Or does he have better balance and outline if his hind legs are not pulled too far back? At what rate of speed, when moving, does he perform his best?

Pretend that you are a judge. Envision the perfect Basset, and employing your knowledge of the standard as a yardstick, study your dog as though he were a strange animal. From this study you will see many things, tiny nuances, that will aid you in showing your Basset to the best possible advantage in open competition.

Once he has mastered the show training you have given him, you must take every opportunity to allow strangers and friends to go over your dog, much in the manner of a judge, while you pose and gait him, so he will become used to a judge's unaccustomed liberties. It would be well to enter your Basset in a few sanction matches now, to acquaint him with the actual conditions under which he will be shown. During all this time, of course, the character and temperament of your dog, as well as his physical assets, must be taken into consideration, as it must in all types of training, and the most made of the best he has.

It is of the utmost importance that you never become blind to your dog's faults, but at the same time realize his good features and attempt to exploit these when in the ring. Make sure your dog is in good physical shape, in good coat, clean and well groomed. If a bath is necessary, give it to him several days before the show so the natural oils will have time to smooth the coat and give it a natural sheen. Be sure he is not thirsty when he enters the ring and that he has emptied himself before showing, or it will cramp his movement and make him uncomfortable.

School yourself to be at ease in the ring when handling your dog, for if you are tense and nervous, it will communicate itself to the dog, and he will display the same emotional stress. In the ring, keep one eye on your dog and the other on the judge. One never knows when a judge might turn from the animal he is examining, look at your dog, and perhaps catch him in an awkward moment.

On the morning of the show, leave your home early enough so that you will have plenty of time to be benched and tend to any last minute details which may come up. When the class before yours is in the ring, give your dog a last quick brush, then run a towel over his coat to bring out the gloss. Should his coat be dull, a few drops of brilliantine, rubbed between the palms of your hands and then sparingly applied to the dog's coat, will aid in eliminating the dullness.

Bring to the show with you: a water pail, towel, brush, suppositories in a small jar, a bench chain, and a light leash for showing. If the dog has not emptied himself, insert a suppository in his rectum when you take him to the exercising ring. If you forgot to bring the suppositories, use instead two paper matches, wet with saliva, from which you have removed the sulphur tips.

Following is a chart listing the dog-show classes and indicating eligibility in each class, with appropriate remarks. This chart will tell you at a glance which is the best class for your dog.

CLASSES AND JUDGING

DOG-SHOW CLASS CHART

CLASS	ELIGIBLE DOGS	REMARKS
PUPPY—6 months and under 9 months	All puppies from 6 months up to 9 months.	Imports (except Canadian) not eligible for this class.

This excellent champion Basset stud dog, Prince Albert of Palos Verde, owned by Virginia Merrimer (same dog used in two former shots) is shown holding show pose without leash.

PUPPY—9 months and under 12 months	All puppies from 9 months to 12 months.	Imports (except Canadian) not eligible for this class.
NOVICE	Any dog or puppy which has not won an adult class (over 12 months), or any higher award, at a point show.	After three first-place Novice wins, cannot be shown again in the class. American- or Canadian-bred only.
BRED BY EXHIBITOR	Any dog or puppy, other than a Champion, which is owned and bred by exhibitor.	Must be shown only by owner or a member of immediate family of breeder-exhibitor, *i.e.*, husband, wife, father, mother, son, daughter, brother, sister.
AMERICAN-BRED	All dogs or puppies whelped in the U.S. or possessions, except Champions, from a mating which took place in the U.S.	
OPEN DOGS	All dogs, 6 months of age or over, in cluding Champions and foreign-breds.	Canadian and foreign champions are shown in open until acquisition of American title. By common courtesy, most American Champions are entered only for Best of Breed Competition.
BEST OF BREED COMPETITION	American Champions.	Compete for Best of Breed or Best of Variety, for which no points are given.

Each sex is judged separately. The winners of each class compete against each other for Winners and Reserve Winners. The animal designated as Winners is awarded the points. Reserve Winners receive no points. Reserve Winners can be the second dog in the class from which the Winners Dog was chosen. The Winners Dog and Winners Bitch compete against the Champions for Best of Breed, and the Best of Breed winner goes into the Hound Group. If fortunate enough to top this group, the final step is to compete against the other group winners for the Best in Show title.

After the judge has chosen his Best of Breed winner he must then decide on his Best of Winners. If either the Winners Dog or the Winners Bitch has been chosen Best of Breed the Best of Winners award is automatic. If not, judging for this takes place at this point. Following the judging for Best of Winners the judge chooses the Best of Opposite Sex.

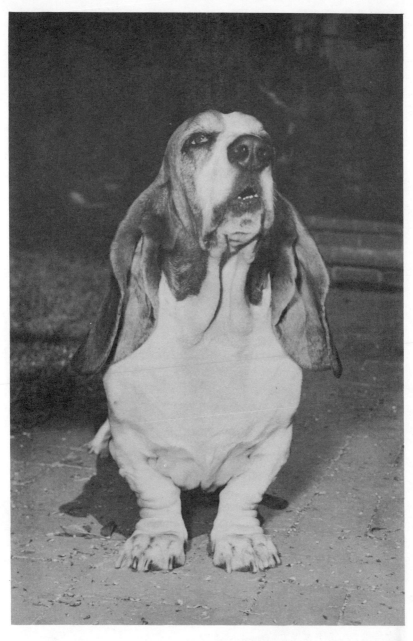

Stacked for show and exhibiting a good
stance in front with lower arms lying
close to chest.

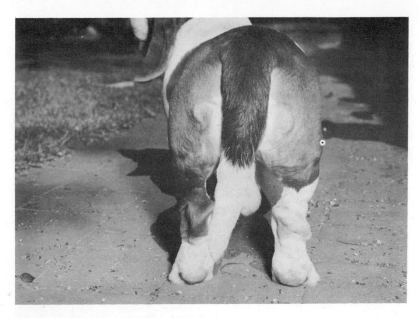

Good rear stance for a male Basset with
the hocks in good alignment. Below,
Ben Harris of Encino, California,
correctly show-stacks his Royal Oaks Gai Lothario.

A dog defeated for Best of Winners is still eligible to compete for Best Opposite, provided it is not of the same sex as the Best of Breed Winner.

Champions are made by the point system. Only the Winners Dog and Winners Bitch receive points, and the amount of points won depends upon the number of Bassets of its own sex the dog has defeated in the classes (not by the number entered). The United States is divided into five regional point groups by the A.K.C., and the point rating varies with the region in which the show is held. Consult a show catalogue for regional rating. A Basset going Best of Winners is allowed the same number of points as the animal of the opposite sex which it defeats if the points are of a greater amount than it won by defeating members of its own sex.

To become a Champion, a dog must win fifteen points under a minimum of three different judges. In accumulating these points, he must win points in at least two major (three points or more) shows, under different judges. Five points is the maximum amount that can be won at any given show. If your Basset wins a group, he is entitled to the highest number of points won in any of the Hound breeds by the dogs he defeats in the group if the points exceed the amount he has won in his own breed. If the show is a Basset Hound Specialty, then the Best of Breed winner automatically becomes the Best in Show dog.

As previously mentioned, Champions compete almost exclusively in the class called "Best of Breed Competition." In addition to dogs whose Championships have been confirmed by the American Kennel Club, the class is opened to dogs who have, according to their owners' records, finished but have not as yet received confirmation. The period that an unconfirmed Champion may compete in this class is limited to 90 days from the time it has acquired its final Championship points.

The basic reason for the dog show, the object in the gathering together of representative animals of the breed in open competition, seems to have been mislaid in the headlong pursuit for ribbons, trophies, and points. These prizes undoubtedly lead to kennel-name popularity, which in turn produces greater and more profitable puppy sales and stud services, but they are not the end in themselves. They are given simply as tokens of achievement in a much larger pattern which has no direct relation to economy. The graded selection of various dogs according to individual quality by a competent, unbiased judge enables earnest breeders to weigh and evaluate the products of certain breedings and strains. It helps them to evaluate their own breeding procedures in relation to comparative quality, and to give them an idea as to which individuals, or breeding lines, can act as correctives to the faults inherent in their own breeding. Here the yardstick of the official standard is used to measure the defects or virtues of individual animals and of the breed as a whole for the edification and tabulation of both the knowing breeder and the novice. This is what a dog show should mean to the exhibitor.

Essentially the judge should be an intermediary between the present and the future, because his decisions shape the trends for better or for worse. If these trends lead to undesirable results, there will be deterioration instead of an ever-closer approach to the breed ideal. The judge is a sounding board, a calculator of degrees of excellence, an instrument for computing worth. He can, with each assignment, give something of enduring value toward breed improvement. As such, he or she must not only be entirely familiar with the standard, but must also understand every element of structure and balance. And almost more important, the judge

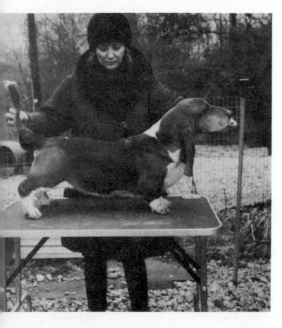

All the time spent in teaching your Basset to pose correctly finally finds fulfillment. Mrs. Leonard Skolnick and the lovely Ch. Slippery Hill Egypt.

must be able to see and evaluate each of those tiny nuances of quality which can establish the superiority of one animal over another of apparently equal excellence.

Though there are times when the judge is at fault, we must not forget that there are many times when the exhibitor's evaluation of the judge's placings is faulty. Too many exhibitors know too little about their own breed and are not competent to indulge in criticism. The very structure of dog-show procedure lends itself to dissatisfaction with the judge's decisions. The fact that there can be only a few really satisfied winners in any breed judging, Winners Dog, Winners Bitch, and Best of Breed, and that they are chosen by one individual who may or may not be competent, leaves a wide range of just or unjust recrimination for the exhibitor to air. Some of the post-mortem denunciations can be attributed directly to the psychological effect of the shows upon the exhibitors themselves.

Many of the most prominent breeders who have been in the breed for years are judges as well. They are frequently criticized for their show-ring placements because they will put up animals of their own breeding or those of similar type to the strain they themselves produce. Undeniably, there are many instances in which a dog, handled or owned by an individual who is himself a judge, is given preference, since the breeder-judge officiating at the moment will, in the near future, show under the owner of the dog he has put up and expects the same consideration in return. This is but one of the many ways in which a judge may be influenced consciously or unconsciously. Regardless of the underlying cause, such practice must be condemned. But in most cases the breeder-judge who elevates animals of his own breeding or dogs of similar type cannot be summarily accused of lack of integrity. The type which he breeds must be the type he likes and his own interpretation of the standard. It follows, therefore, that this is the type he will put up in all honesty. We may question his taste, knowledge, or interpretation of the standard, but not, in most instances, his ethics or honesty.

There are, thank goodness, quite a few qualified and earnest judges whose placings should be followed and analyzed, for it is through them that we can evaluate the breeding health of the Basset and know with confidence the individual worth of specific specimens. Judging is not an easy task. It does not generally lead to long and cozy friendships, for once an individual steps into the ring to begin his judiciary assignment, he is no longer an individual but becomes the impartial, wholly objective instrument of the standard. As such, friendship, personal likes or dislikes, cannot exist as facets of his make-up. He must judge the dogs before him as they are on that day without sentiment or favor. This is a task that demands complete subjection of self, high knowledge of the breed, and courage and integrity. It can be easily seen then, that not too many people could qualify in all these respects and so become completely proficient judges.

Were the ideal condition to exist, we, the breeders and owners, would submit our animals in open competition to the careful scrutiny of a truly competent authority whose integrity was beyond question. We would be able to compare our stock within the ring to see where we had erred. We would be able to measure the worth of breeding theory by the yardstick of a correct interpretation of the standard. We would know then what breeding lines were producing animals closest to the ideal and which individual dogs showed the highest degree of excellence; by thus creating, through

There is no thrill like the one of winning with a
dog that you have trained and handled yourself.

the medium of the judge, an authority which we could depend upon, we could establish an easier path to the breed ideal.

Remember that showing dogs is a sport, not a matter of life and death. Tomorrow is another day, another show, another judge. The path of the show dog is never strewn with roses, though it may look that way to the novice handler who seems, inevitably, to step on thorns. Always be a good sport, don't run the other fellow's dog down because he has beaten yours, and when a Basset goes into the group, give him your hearty applause even if you don't like the dog, his handler, his owner, and his breeding. Remember only that he is Basset Hound, a representative of your breed and therefore the best dog in the group.

We hope that this chapter will help the novice show handler to find greater ease and surety in training for show and handling in the ring and thus experience more pleasure from exhibiting. Competition is the spice of life, and a good Basset Hound should be shown to his best advantage, for his own glory and for the greater benefit of the breed.

The bawling, haunting voice of a Basset in the
field on a crisp day has no parallel in dogdom.

CHAPTER XII

Basic Field Training

Your Basset Hound is bred to hunt slowly and carefully, and his superb scenting ability, unequaled except by the Bloodhound, is a part of the intricate heredity he possesses that makes him such a fine field dog. He is a gentle dog, fairly easy to train but slow and deliberate and extremely determined on the trail. His remarkable scenting ability makes him reluctant to accept any fact except one that his nose tells him is so. He will, in fact, follow the scent of any creature he wishes to approach even though it is in plain sight; his reliance is on his scenting ability rather than any other of his senses.

Your Basset cannot be pushed and will react slowly and deliberately to your commands. He is a natural trailer and will push through any cover stubbornly on his short legs, keeping to the scent line. On trail he will make his own deliberate decisions in his own uniquely unhurried way.

Some strains of Bassets inherit the ability to start training earlier than others but the earlier you can begin training with any hope of success, the better. Generally speaking training can begin at about four to five months. We will assume that your puppy is leash and collar broken before you take him into the field. Some of the basic obedience commands should also have been learned by the tyro before he is exposed to the hunting atmosphere, namely the commands "Come," and "Sit." You must also make sure at this time that the puppy can differentiate between play and training. Play is boisterous, gay, and without much restriction; training is pleasant and requires attention.

In all training, including field training, control and understanding of both the drives and limitations of the pupil is necessary. A rapport must be established between trainer and pupil, a feeling of oneness and, when this occurs, then training becomes easy and pleasurable for both.

To begin, take your puppy out into the woods and let him poke around and get the feel of woods, field and stream so that he learns how to navigate and becomes accustomed to this new environment. Call him back to you occasionally and tell him to sit in front of you, then release him again. It will be a fun outing and he will associate the field with pleasant things and wonderful new smells that pique and stir his ancestral memory.

After a few of these outings begin using a simple drag doctored with rabbit training scent. The scent will excite him and he will begin to trail

Five Couple of Basset Hounds of the Coldstream
Bassets; joint masters, Mr. and Mrs. Joseph J.
McKenna.

and, in the process, learn a new command, "Seek," or "Hunt," or "Get it." Follow behind and urge him forward. Never allow him to run the line back, or "back-trail." If he does you will be there to scold or punish him with your voice, indicating your displeasure. Set him going forward again and praise him when he follows the scent correctly. Don't expect him to follow exactly on the scent line always, because wind-drift can sometimes cause the pup to trail a short distance off the direct line you have laid. Actually you will not be training your Basset in the strict sense of the term; rather will you be allowing your hound to develop the natural tendencies that are his heritage.

As soon as your Basset runs a scent line nicely it is time to introduce him to live game. Most trainers use a tame rabbit for this initial encounter. An assistant releases the rabbit in sight of the puppy and, as the rabbit hops away, the owner or trainer releases the youngster and encourages him to chase the rabbit, using the same commands as he did previously when the drag was used.

After a few minutes of backing and chasing of the rabbit by the young dog, the rabbit is caught up and returned to its pen and the pup is praised mightily for his, we hope, vigorous and discerning action. Now the puppy should be immediately taken to a field and started on a wild rabbit. To make sure that game will be there and available to the youngster's attention, a pen housing a wild rabbit should have been earlier hidden in the brush. Again we must use our assistant, this time to hide where the pen is and release the wild rabbit so it can be seen by the Basset puppy. The chase begins again with the accompaniment of much loud encouragement by the trainer.

Some trainers, who feel that they have a very apt pupil, eliminate these steps entirely and move directly from working the puppy on the drag to the field and allow the pupil to pick up his own trail. It must, of course, be an area where wild rabbits abound and a trail can be easily found. Stay close and give the youngster a lot of encouragement, using the same words of command as you did on the drag. If you have, or can borrow, an older well-broken hound to run with your youngster it can help him immeasurably. He must be a friendly, oldish type, quiet and willing with years of experience behind him and no faults that can be picked up by the puppy. Do NOT use a fast, aggressive young dog as a tutor. He will only confuse your puppy and make negative all that you have achieved thus far.

Your puppy should have been long accustomed to the sound of a gun but, if he isn't, use a light .22 at first, when he is eating and from a distance. Then use it when he is eagerly and completely immersed in trailing. Gradually move closer until it can be shot quite close to your Basset. Either a rifle or a .22 target or training pistol will do the trick using blanks, of course. Introduce the shotgun in the same way then, when you feel that the dog is ready to have the kill made, shoot the game far enough ahead of the trailing dog so that he won't become alarmed but close enough so that he will be able to associate the sound of the shot with the freshly killed game.

Hounds can acquire faults even if used always alone. When this happens it is good sense to use a brace-mate to correct such bad habits as cutting up on line or straying from checks, etc. Often a hound that doesn't indicate enough enthusiasm for field work can be given incentive by working with a pack. Some of the engendered excitement will undoubtedly rub off.

Basset Hound owners and trainers have very little to worry about so far as the voice of their hounds is concerned. One seldom finds a tight-mouthed Basset. But, if you have the exception, again packing will develop enough excitement in the hound to make him open up with more fervor. Incidentally, the voice of a Basset Hound on game on a cool frosty night is an unforgettable experience. The clear, bell-like tones will live in your memory as a pleasurable experience for the rest of your life.

If you wish to use your Basset Hound on pheasants (and Bassets make excellent pheasant dogs), use a wing-clipped bird. If he fails after a good try, accept it. Even a fair degree of success initially is heartening when breaking your dog to pheasant. They are not easy to find and, unlike most wounded birds, they leave very little scent. When your Basset has become accomplished in this area you will be amazed at how great he is on runners. This is where his fantastic powers of scent make him invaluable.

Basset Hounds, to a greater degree than many other of the scent-hound breeds, have a natural retrieving aptitude. Many trainers prefer to use dead game first or a dummy, in training to retrieve. But, as mentioned above, Bassets have a natural instinct for this chore. Most dogs will mouth the game that is shot over, or in front of, them. Encourage your Basset to pick it up then, using the code word "Bring," or "Fetch," urge the dog to carry the game as you back away, holding your hand out. Don't back too far or your dog will lose interest in reaching you before he drops the game.

When you have gotten him to pick up the game and come toward your outstretched hand, command him to "Sit" in front of you holding the game and reach out to take it from him. Generally he will drop it as you hold out your hand, but once he does it a few times correctly and is properly praised he will retain the game in his mouth and release it to your hand. Be gentle when taking it from his mouth; don't pull or handle it roughly or he will become hard-mouthed. As in all training, never play with your dog when teaching him to retrieve and always demand (and get) a clean delivery.

If the pupil absolutely refuses to retrieve the game, tie your handkerchief around the body of the bird or rabbit and throw it out for him to retrieve as he did the dummy (if you used a dummy in the early steps of his training). Your body scent on the handkerchief will generally make the dog willing to mouth the game.

Your Basset Hound can enrich your life immeasurably through the age-old medium of the hunting field. If he is a house pet, or a show dog, remember that he is also a sporting dog and that both of you can find pleasure together in nature's own back yard doing what man did when the race was young. In the woods and fields with your Basset by your side or bawling on a hot trail, your everyday tensions will slip away, anxieties will fade and you will be whole again, made so by the peace that has come to be, at that moment, within you.

Yes, it is worthwhile to train your Basset to take up his heritage. Most trainers will tell you that all the knowledge they have gleaned over the years in training for field trial work or as a gentleman's hunting companion was gained in the shooting field. Only there will you experience

This litter, out of Engle's Xmas Cheer and Tulpehocken Shorty, produced three Field Champions. Five weeks old in this photo, they represent an average-size litter.

Training your Basset to ride well in your car is
a necessary part of field training.

the countless hound peculiarities that you must overcome in basic training. It is this knowledge beyond the ordinary that lifts such training
from the category of the mundane and ordinary and makes of it an art.

There are quite a few field trials for Bassets held each year throughout
the country. Entries are small per dog per stake and information on
when and where the trials are being held can be furnished you by the
Basset Hound Club of America. All classes are divided by sex and there
are classes for both experienced field trail hounds and novices. The trials
follow the same procedure as do Beagle trials; two entries are run together
for each brace and, at the beginning of each brace run the spectators
spread out and move through the field and "walk up" a rabbit. The competing brace hounds are kept leashed and turned loose together on the
fresh scent when the rabbit is started. The names or numbers of the dogs
that will form each brace are drawn blind, by lot. Only the handlers and

Dr. Leonard Skolnick posing one of his fine field
trial Champions, Slippery Hill Calvin. Below is
Mrs. Lynwood Walton with the excellent Basset
Ch. Lyn-Mar's Clown. The Lyn-Mar Kennels
(Lyn-Mar Acres), owned by Mr. and Mrs.
Lynwood Walton, Mount Holly, N.J., are
nationally known for their fine stock.

Ed Eylander with Field Ch. Ed's Jo Jo, John N. Eylander with Field Ch. Max's Happy Hunter, and John Eylander, Jr. handling Eylander's Shortstop. All the Bassets are owned by John N. Eylander, who was president of the National Club in the '60s.

judges are allowed to closely follow the competing hounds the spectators; or gallery, stay back so that they will not interfere with the work of the hounds. The judges give all the directions during the running and the handlers of the hounds are not allowed to give their dogs any assistance except when directed to do so by the judge.

Any purebred Basset Hound who is eligible for A.K.C. registration and is six months or more of age may compete. If the entry is large enough points are awarded to the first three hounds and, as in the show ring, points toward a championship (field trial) are awarded based on the number of hounds competing.

More and more Basset Hound breeders and owners are becoming aware of and enamored of the field trial. Consequently the size of Basset Hound field trials has grown by leaps and bounds. It's healthy for both man and beast and is also good fun for both and you will be in the company of the finest people in the world, that exclusive group known as "Dog People."

Ch. Look's Musical of Musicland.

CHAPTER XIII

Diseases and First Aid

The dog is heir to many illnesses, and, as with man, it seems that when one dread form has been overcome by some specific medical cure, another quite as lethal takes its place. It is held by some that this cycle will always continue, since it is nature's basic way of controlling population.

There are, of course, several ways to circumvent Dame Nature's lethal plans. The initial step in this direction is to put the health of your dogs in the hands of one who has the knowledge and equipment, mental and physical, to competently cope with your canine health problems. We mean, of course, a modern veterinarian. Behind this man are years of study and experience and a knowledge of all the vast research, past and present, which has developed the remarkable cures and artificial immunities that have so drastically lowered the canine mortality rate as of today.

Put your trust in the qualified veterinarian and "beware of Greeks bearing gifts." Beware, too, of helpful friends who say, "I know what the trouble is and how to cure it. The same thing happened to my dog." Home doctoring by unskilled individuals acting upon the advice of unqualified "experts" has killed more dogs than distemper.

Your Basset is constantly exposed to innumerable diseases through the medium of flying and jumping insects, parasites, bacteria, fungus, and virus. His body develops defenses and immunities against many of these diseases, but there are many more which we must cure or immunize him against if they are not to prove fatal.

I am not qualified to give advice about treatment for the many menaces to your dog's health that exist and, by the same token, you are not qualified to treat your dog for these illnesses with the skill or knowledge necessary for success. I can only give you a resumé of modern findings on the most prevalent diseases and illnesses so that you can, in some instances, eliminate them or the causative agent yourself. Even more important, this chapter will help you recognize their symptoms in time to seek the aid of your veterinarian.

Though your dog can contract disease at any time or any place, he or she is most greatly exposed to danger when in the company of other dogs at dog shows or in a boarding kennel. Watch your dog carefully after it has been hospitalized or sent afield to be bred. Many illnesses have an incubation period, during the early stages of which the animal himself

For your Basset's sake, put your faith in a good
veterinarian. He has been painstakingly trained
to care for your dog medically.

may not show the symptoms of the disease, but can readily contaminate other dogs with which he comes in contact. It is readily seen, then, that places where many dogs are gathered together, such as those mentioned above, are particularly dangerous to your dog's health.

Parasitic diseases, which we will first investigate, must not be taken too lightly, though they are the easiest of the diseases to cure. Great suffering and even death can come to your dog through these parasites that prey on him if you neglect to realize the importance of both cure and the control of reinfestation.

EXTERNAL PARASITES

The lowly flea is one of the most dangerous insects from which you must protect your dog. It carries and spreads tapeworm, heartworm, and bubonic plague, causes loss of coat and weight, spreads skin disease, and brings untold misery to its poor host. These pests are particularly difficult to combat because their eggs—of which they lay thousands—can lie dormant for months, hatching when conditions of moisture and warmth are present. Thus you may think you have rid your dog (and your house) of these devils, only to find that they mysteriously reappear as weather conditions change.

When your dog has fleas, use any good commercial flea powder which contains fresh rotenone. Dust him freely with the powder. It is not necessary to cover the dog completely, since the flea is active and will quickly reach a spot saturated with the powder and die. Rotenone is also fatal to lice. A solution of this drug in pine oil and added to water to be employed as a dip or rinse will kill all insects except ticks. DDT in liquid soap is excellent and long-potent, its effect lasting for as long as a week. Benzene hexochloride, chlordane, and any number of many new insecticides developed for the control of flies are also lethal to fleas. Whatever specific

Remember your Basset can pick up parasites and disease from other pets. If he does, see your veterinarian immediately.

is prescribed by your veterinarian should also be used on your dog's sleeping quarters as well as on the animal itself. Repeat the treatment in ten days to eliminate fleas which have been newly hatched from dormant eggs.

Chlorinated hydrocarbons (DDT, chlordane, dieldrin, etc.) are long acting. Organic phosphoriferous substances, such as Malathion, are quick killers with no lasting effect.

TICKS

There are many kinds of ticks, all of which go through similar stages in their life process. At some stage in their lives they all find it necessary to feed on blood. Luckily, these pesty vampires are fairly easily controlled. The female of the species is much larger than the male, which will generally be found hiding under the female. Care must be taken in the removal of these pests to guard against the mouth parts remaining embedded in the host's skin when the body of the tick is removed. DDT is an effective tick remover. Ether or nail-polish remover, touched to the individual tick, will cause it to relax its grip and fall off the host. The heated head of a match from which the flame has been just extinguished,

Specific liquid medication being applied to a
"hot" spot with an eyedropper.

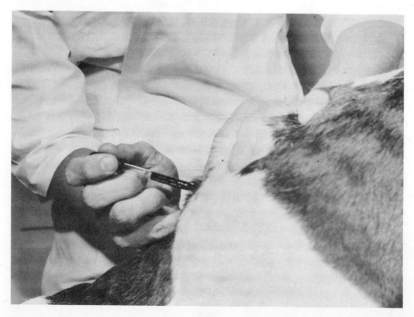

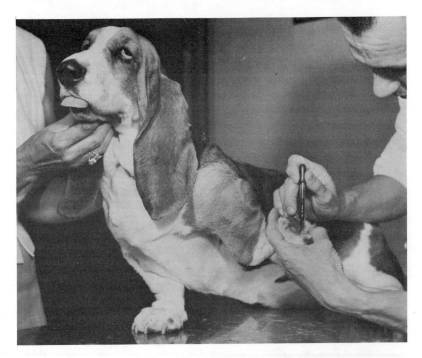

An eyedropper can also be employed for administering medication between the toes.

employed in the same fashion, will cause individual ticks to release their hold and fall from the dog. After veterinary tick treatment, no attempt should be made to remove the pests manually, since the treatment will cause them to drop by themselves as they succumb. Chlorinated hydrocarbons are very effective tick removers.

MITES

There are three basic species of mites that generally infect dogs, the demodectic mange mite (red mange), the sarcoptic mange mite (white mange), and the ear mite. Demodectic mange is generally recognized by balding areas on the face, cheeks, and the front parts of the forelegs, which present a moth-eaten appearance. Reddening of the skin and great irritation occurs as a result of the frantic rubbing and scratching of affected parts by the animal. Rawness and thickening of the skin follows. Not too long ago this was a dread disease in dogs, from which few recovered. It is still a persistent and not easily cured condition unless promptly diagnosed and diligently attended to.

Ch. Coralwoods Kadiddlehopper, top winning Basset in the 70s, shown by owner and breeder Wm. Barton of Coralwood Kennels, Judge Dr. Skolnick.

Sarcoptic mange mites can infest you as well as your dog. The resulting disease is known as scabies. This disease very much resembles dry dermatitis, or what is commonly called "dry eczema." The coat falls out and the denuded area becomes inflamed and itches constantly.

Ear mites*, of course, infest the dog's ear and can be detected by an accumulation of crumbly dark brown or black wax within the ear. Shaking of the head and frequent scratching at the site of the infestation accompanied by squeals and grunting also is symptomatic of the presence of these pests. Canker of the ear is a condition, rather than a specific disease, which covers a wide range of ear infection and which displays symptoms similar to ear mite infection.

All three of these diseases and ear canker should be treated by your veterinarian. By taking skin scrapings or wax particles from the ear for microscopic examination, he can make an exact diagnosis and recommend specific treatment. The irritations caused by these ailments, unless immediately controlled, can result in loss of appetite and weight, and so lower your dog's natural resistance that he is open to the attack of other diseases which his bodily defenses could normally battle successfully.

INTERNAL PARASITES

It seems strange, in the light of new discovery of specific controls for parasitism, that the incidence of parasitic infestation should still be almost as great as it was years ago. This can only be due to lack of realization by the dog owner of the importance of initial prevention and control against reinfestation. Strict hygiene must be adhered to if dogs properly treated are not to be exposed to infestation immediately again. This is particularly true where worms are concerned.

In attempting to rid our dogs of worms, we must not be swayed by amateur opinion. The so-called "symptoms" of worms may be due to many other reasons. We may see the actual culprits in the animal's stool, but even then it is not wise to worm indiscriminately. The safest method to pursue is to take a small sample of your dog's stool to your veterinarian. By a fecal analysis he can advise just what specific types of worms infest your dog and what drugs should be used to eliminate them.

Do not worm your dog because you "*think*" he should be wormed, or because you are advised to do so by some self-confessed "authority." Drugs employed to expel worms can prove highly dangerous to your dog if used indiscriminately and carelessly, and in many instances the same symptoms that are indicative of the presence of internal parasites can also be the signs of some other affliction.

* Otodectic mange.

178

A word here in regard to that belief that garlic will "cure" worms. Garlic is an excellent flavoring agent, favored by gourmets the world over—but—it will not rid your dog of worms. Its only curative power lies in the fact that, should you use it on a housedog who has worms, the first time he pants in your face you will definitely be cured of ever attempting this pseudo-remedy again.

ROUNDWORM

These are the most common worms found in dogs and can have great effects upon puppies, which they almost invariably infest. Potbellies, general unthriftiness, diarrhea, coughing, lack of appetite, anemia, are the symptons. They can also cause verminous pneumonia when in the larvae stage. Fecal examination of puppy stools should be made by your veterinarian frequently if control of these parasites is to be constant.

1. Flea-host tapeworm. 2. Segment of tapeworm as seen in dog's stool. 3. Common roundworm. 4. Whipworm. 5. Hookworm. 6. Heartworm.

Although theoretically it is possible for small puppies to be naturally worm free, actually most pups are born infested or contract the parasitic eggs at the mother's breast.

The roundworm lives in the intestine and feeds on the dog's partially digested food, growing and laying eggs which are passed out in the dog's stool to be picked up by him in various ways and so cause reinfestation. The life history of all the intestinal worms is a vicious circle, with the dog the beginning and the end host. This worm is yellowish-white in color and is shaped like a common garden worm, pointed at both ends. It is usually curled when found in the stool. There are several different species of this type of worm. Some varieties are more dangerous than others. They discharge toxin within the dog, and the movement of larvae to important internal sections of the dog's body can cause death.

The two drugs most used by kennel owners for the elimination of roundworms are N-butyl-chloride and tetrachloroethylene, but there are a host of other drugs, new and old, that can also do the job efficiently. With most of the worm drugs, give no food to the dog for twenty-four hours, or in the case of puppies, twenty hours, previous to the time he is given the medicine. It is absolutely essential that this starvation limit be adhered to, particularly if the drug used is tetrachloroethylene, since the existence of the slightest amount of food in the stomach or intestine can cause death. One tenth c.c. to each pound of the animal's weight is the dosage for tetrachloroethylene, followed in one hour with a milk-of-magnesia physic, *never* an oily physic. Food may be given two hours later.

N-butyl-chloride is less toxic if the dog has eaten some food during the supposed starvation period. The dosage is one c.c. for every ten pounds of the weight of the dog. Any safe physic may be administered an hour later, and the dog fed within two hours afterwards. Large doses of this drug can be given grown dogs without danger, and will kill whipworms as well as roundworms. A second treatment should follow in two weeks. The effect of N-butyl-chloride is accumulative; therefore, when a large dosage is necessary, the total amount to be given can be divided into many small doses administered, one small dose at a time, over a period of hours. The object of this procedure is to prevent the dog from vomiting up the drug, which generally occurs when a large dose is given all at once. This method of administering the drug has been found to be very effective.

A new product, *piperazine*, available in several forms and marketed under various brand names, is the latest efficient roundworm specific. It can be given in food, and eliminates the need for the starving period. In fact it will soon be sold incorporated in dog food or biscuits. Semi-annual usage in kennels could in time practically eliminate this scourge from dogdom.

HOOKWORMS

These tiny leeches who live on the blood of your dog, which they get from the intestinal walls, cause severe anemia, groaning, fits, diarrhea, loss of appetite and weight, rapid breathing, and swelling of the legs. The same drugs, and tolkuene, used to eradicate roundworms will also expel hookworms.

Good food is essential for quick recovery, with added amounts of liver and raw meat incorporated in the diet. Blood transfusions are often necessary if the infestation has been heavy. If one infestation follows another, a certain degree of immunity to the effects of the parasite seems to be built up by the dog. A second treatment should be given two weeks following the initial treatment.

Author's note: There are several new medical inoculations to rid your dog of, or control, external and internal parasites (fleas and the various worms).

WHIPWORMS

These small, thin whiplike worms are found in the intestines and the caecum. Those found in the intestines are reached and killed by the same drugs used in the eradication of roundworms and hookworms. Most worm medicines will kill these helminths if they reach them, but those which live in the caecum are very difficult to reach. They exude toxins which cause debilitation, anemia, and allied ills, and are probably a contributing factor in lowering the resistance to the onslaught of other infections. The usual symptoms of worm infestation are present.

N-butyl-chloride, in dosage three times greater than the roundworm dosage, appears to be quite effective in reaching the caecum and ridding the dog of most of these pests. The drug is to be given following the twenty-four hour period of fasting. Administration of an anti-emetic is generally indicated to keep the dog from disgorging the drug.

Phthalofyne is an effective whipworm eradicator that can be administered by either intravenous injection or by oral tablets.

TAPEWORMS

Tapeworms are not easily diagnosed by fecal test, but are easily identi-

The veterinarian is shown in this photograph in the act of administering a worm pill to a patient.

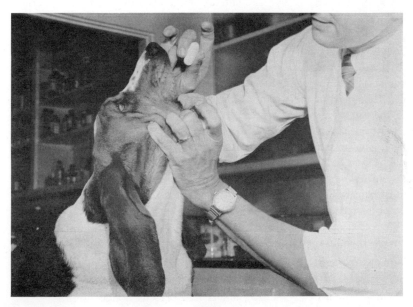

181

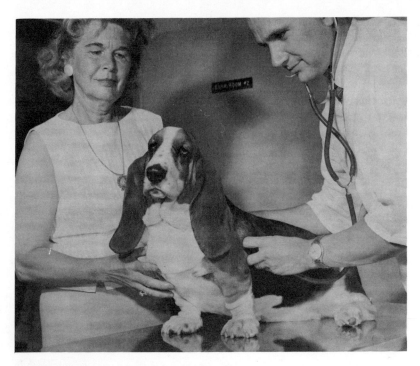

Veterinarian checking the heart of a Basset.

fied when visible in the dog's stool. The worm is composed of two distinct parts, the head and the segmented body. It is pieces of the segmented body that we see in the stools of the dog. They are usually pink or white in color and flat. The common tapeworm, which is most prevalent in our dogs, is about eighteen inches long, and the larvae are carried by the flea. The head of the worm is smaller than a pinhead and attaches itself to the intestinal wall. Contrary to general belief, the dog infested with tapeworms does not possess an enormous appetite—rather it fluctuates from good to poor. The animal shows the general signs of worm infestation. Often he squats and drags his hindquarters on the ground. This is due to tapeworm larvae moving and wriggling in the lower bowels. One must be careful in diagnosing this symptom, as it may also mean that the dog is suffering from distended anal glands.

Arecolene is an efficient expeller of tapeworms. Dosage is approximately one-tenth grain for every fifteen pounds of the dog's weight, administered after twenty hours of fasting. Nemural is also widely used. One pill for every eight pounds of body weight is given in a small amount of food after twelve hours of starvation. No worm medicine can be considered 100 per cent effective in all cases. If one drug does not expel the worms satis-factorily, then another must be tried.

HEARTWORM

This villain inhabits the heart and is the most difficult to treat. The worm is about a foot long and literally stuffs the heart of the affected animal. It is prevalent in the southern states and has long been the curse of sporting-dog breeds. The worm is transmitted principally through the bite of an infected mosquito, which can fly from an infected southern canine visitor directly to your northern Basset and do its dire deed.

The symptoms are: fatigue, gasping, coughing, nervousness, and some-times dropsy and swelling of the extremities. Treatment for heartworms definitely must be left in the hands of your veterinarian. A wide variety of drugs are used in treatment; the most commonly employed are the arsenicals, antimony compounds, and caracide. Danger exists during cure when dying adult worms move to the lungs, causing suffocation, or

Only a healthy dog can have that glow and the
energy that makes for field or show winning.

when dead microfilariae, in a heavily infested dog, block the small blood vessels in the heart muscles. The invading microfilariae are not discernible in the blood until nine months following introduction of the disease by the bite of the carrier mosquito.

In an article on this subject in *Field & Stream* magazine, Joe Stetson describes a controlled experiment in which caracide was employed in periodic treatments as a preventative of heartworm. The experiment was carried out over a period of eighteen months, during which time the untreated dogs became positive for heartworm and eventually died. A post mortem proved the presence of the worm. The dogs that underwent scheduled prophylaxis have been found, by blood test, to be free of circulating microfilariae and are thriving.

COCCIDIOSIS

This disease is caused by a single-celled protozoa. It affects dogs of all ages, but is not dangerous to mature animals. When puppies become infected by a severe case of coccidiosis, it very often proves fatal, since it produces such general weakness and emaciation that the puppy has no defense against other invading harmful organisms. Loose and bloody stools are indicative of the presence of this disease, as is loss of appetite, weakness, emaciation, discharge from the eyes, and a fever of approximately 103 degrees. The disease is contracted directly or through flies that have come from infected quarters. Infections seem to occur over and over again, limiting the puppy's chance of recovery with each succeeding infection. The duration of the disease is about three weeks, but new infestations can stretch this period of illness on until your puppy has little chance to recover. Strict sanitation and supportive treatment of good nutrition—utilizing milk, fat, kaopectate, and bone ash, with added dextrose and calcium— seem to be all that can be done in the way of treatment. Force feed the puppy if necessary. The more food that you can get into him to give him strength until the disease has run its course, the better will be his chances of recovery. Specific cures have been developed in other animals and poultry, but not as yet in dogs. Recovered dogs are life-long carriers of the disease. Sulfamethazine may give some control.

SKIN DISEASES

Diseases of the skin in dogs are many, varied, and easily confused by the kennel owner as to category. All skin afflictions should be immediately diagnosed by your veterinarian so that treatment can begin with dispatch. Whatever drug is prescribed must be employed diligently and in quantity

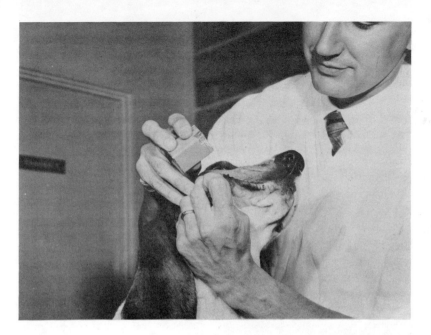

Administering liquid medication. Note that the
veterinarian uses the natural lip pouch as funnel.

and generally long after surface indication of the disease has ceased to
exist. A surface cure may be attained, but the infection remains buried
deep in the hair follicles or skin glands, to erupt again if treatment is
suspended too soon. Contrary to popular belief, diet, if well balanced
and complete, is seldom the cause of skin disease.

Eczema

The word "eczema" is a much-abused word, as is the word "dermatitis."
Both are used with extravagance in the identification of various forms of
skin disorders. We will concern ourselves with the two most prevalent
forms of so-called eczema, namely wet eczema and dry eczema. In the wet
form, the skin exudes moisture and then scabs over, due to constant
scratching and biting by the dog at the site of infection. The dry form
manifests itself in dry patches which irritate and itch, causing great discomfort to the dog. In both instances the hair falls out and the spread of
the disease is rapid. The cause of these diseases is not yet known, though
many are thought to be originated by various fungi and aggravated by
allergic conditions. The quickest means of bringing these diseases under
control is through the application of a good skin remedy often combined
with a fungicide, which your veterinarian will prescribe. An over-all dip,
employing specific liquid medication, is beneficial in many cases and has

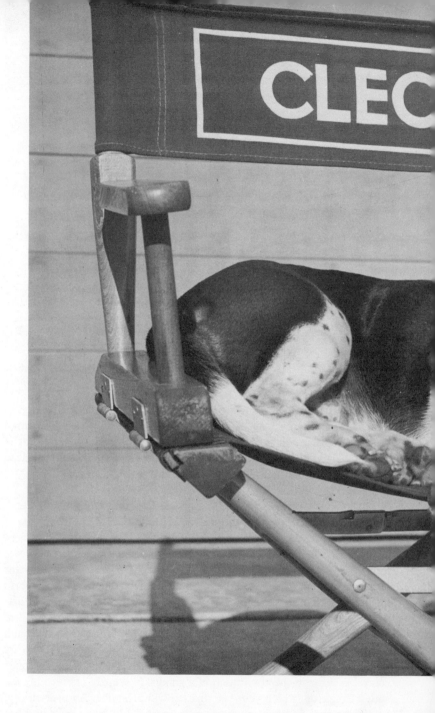

Cleo the TV star takes her ease between
scenes in her own special chair.

a continuing curative effect over a period of days. Injectable or oral anti-inflammatory drugs are supplementary treatment.

Ringworm

This infection is caused by a fungus and is highly contagious to humans. In the dog it generally appears on the face as a round or oval spot from which the hair has fallen. Ringworm is easily cured by the application of iodine glycerine (50 per cent of each ingredient) or a fungicide, such as girseofulvin, liberally applied.

Acne

Your puppy will frequently display small eruptions on the soft skin of his belly. These little pimples rupture and form a scab. The rash is caused by inflammation of the skin glands and is not a serious condition. Treatment consists of washing the affected area with alcohol or witch hazel, followed by the application of a healing lotion or powder. Hormonal imbalances can also cause specific skin conditions that are best left to the administrations of your veterinarian.

Hookworm Larvae Infection

The skin of your dog can become infected from the eggs and larvae of the hookworm acquired from muddy hookworm-infested runs. The larvae become stuck to his coat with mud and burrow into the skin, leaving ugly raw red patches. One or two baths in warm water to which an antiseptic has been added usually cures the condition quickly.

DEFICIENCY DISEASES

These diseases, or conditions, are caused by dietary deficiencies or some condition which robs the diet of necessary ingredients. Anemia, a deficiency condition, is a shortage of hemoglobin. Hookworms, lice, and any disease that depletes the system of red blood cells, are contributory causes. A shortage or lack of specific minerals or vitamins in the diet can also cause anemia. Not so long ago, rickets was the most common of the deficiency diseases, caused by a lack of one or more of the dietary elements—vitamin D, calcium, and phosphorus. There are other types of deficiency diseases originating in dietary inadequacy and characterized by unthriftiness in one or more phases. The cure exists in supplying the missing food factors to the diet. Sometimes, even though all the necessary dietary elements are present in the food, some are destroyed by improper feeding procedure. For example, a substance in raw eggs, avertin, destroys biotin, one of the B-complex group of vitamins. Cooking will destroy the avertin in the egg white and prevent a biotin deficiency in the diet.

Bassets make marvelous pets for young or old,
but they must be kept healthy
to fulfill this role.

Arrange with your veterinarian for a series of protective shots while the pups are young.

BACTERIAL DISEASES

In this group we find leptospirosis, tetanus, pneumonia, strep infections, and many other dangerous diseases. The mortality rate is generally high in all of the bacterial diseases, and treatment should be left to your veterinarian.

Leptospirosis

Leptospirosis is spread most frequently by the urine of infected dogs, which can infect for six months or more after the animal has recovered from the disease. Rats are the carriers of the bacterial agent which produces this disease. A dog will find a bone upon which an infected rat has urinated, chew the bone, and become infested with the disease in turn. Leptospirosis is primarily dangerous in the damage it does to the kidneys. Complete isolation of affected individuals to keep the disease from spreading and rat control of kennel areas are the chief means of prevention. Also, leptospirosis vaccines may be employed by your veterinarian as a preventative measure. Initial diagnosis is difficult, and the disease has generally made drastic inroads before a cure is effected. It has been estimated that fully 50 per cent of all dogs throughout the world have been stricken with leptospirosis at one time or another and that in many instances the disease was not recognized for what it was. The disease produced by *Leptospira* in the blood of humans is known as Weil's disease.

190

Tetanus

Lockjaw bacteria produce an exceedingly deadly poision. The germs grow in the depths of a sealed-over wound where oxygen cannot penetrate. To prevent this disease, every deep wound acquired by your dog should be thoroughly cleansed and disinfected, and an antitoxin given the animal. Treatment follows the same general pattern as prevention. If the jaw locks, intravenous feeding must be given.

Strep throat

This is a very contagious disease caused by a specific group of bacteria labeled "streptococcus." Characteristic of this disease is the high temperature that accompanies infection (104 to 106 degrees). Other symptoms are loose stool at the beginning of the disease and a slight optic discharge. The throat becomes intensely inflamed, swallowing is difficult, and the glands under the ears are swollen. Immunity is developed by the host after the initial attack.

Tonsillitis

Inflammation of the tonsils can be either of bacterial or virus origin. It is not a serious disease in itself, but is often a symptom of other diseases. Tonsillitis is not to be confused with strep throat, which is produced by an entirely different organism. The symptoms of tonsillitis are enlarged and

A healthy dog is an energetic and good working dog. This Basset, in advanced Obedience, must be checked regularly to keep him in condition.

reddened tonsils, poor appetite, vomiting, and optic discharge. The disease usually runs its course in from five to seven days. Penicillin, aureomycin, terramycin, chloromycetin, etc., have been used with success in treatment.

Pneumonia

Pneumonia is a bacterial disease of the lungs of which the symptoms are poor appetite, optic discharge, shallow and rapid respiration. Affected animals become immune to the particular type of pneumonia from which they have recovered. Oral treatment utilizing antibiotic or sulfa drugs, combined with a pneumonia jacket of cloth or cotton padding wrapped around the chest area, seems to be standard treatment.

VIRUS DISEASES

The dread virus diseases are caused by the smallest organisms known to man. They live in the cells and often attack the nerve tissue. The tissue thus weakened is easily invaded by many types of bacteria. Complications then set in, and it is these accompanying ills which usually prove fatal. The secondary infections can be treated with several of the "wonder" drugs, and excellent care and nursing is necessary if the stricken animal is to survive. Your veterinarian is the only person qualified to aid your dog when a virus disease strikes. The diseases in this category include distemper, infectious hepatitis, rabies, kennel cough, and primary encephalitis—the latter actually inflammation of the brain, a condition characterizing several illnesses, particularly those of virus origin.

Distemper

Until recently a great many separate diseases had been lumped under the general heading of distemper. In the last few years modern science has isolated a number of separate diseases of the distemper complex, such as infectious hepatitis, hard-pad disease, influenza, and primary encephalitis, which had been diagnosed as distemper. Thus, with more accurate diagnosis, great strides have been made in conquering, not only distemper, but these other allied diseases. Distemper (Carre) is no longer prevalent due to successful methods of immunization, but any signs of illness in an animal not immunized may be the beginning of the disease. The symptoms are so similar to those of various other diseases that only a trained observer can diagnose correctly. Treatment consists of the use of drugs to counteract complications arising from the invasion of secondary diseases and in keeping the stricken animal warm, well fed, comfortable and free from dehydration until the disease has run its course. In many instances, even if the dog gets well, he will be left with some dreadful souvenir of the disease which will mar him for life. After-effects are common in most of the diseases of the distemper complex.

The tremendous value of immunization against this virus disease cannot be exaggerated. Except for the natural resistance your animal carries against disease, it is the one means of protection you have against this killer. There have been various methods of immunization developed in the last several years, combining several vaccines in one. The human measles vaccine developed to protect very young puppies is highly effective. With the normal vaccine injections can be given at any age, even as early as six or eight weeks, with a repeat dosage at six months of age. It does not affect the tissues, nor can it cause any ill effects to other dogs in a kennel who come in contact with the vaccinated animal.

Infectious hepatitis

This disease attacks dogs of all ages, but is particularly deadly to puppies.

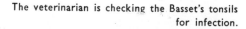

The veterinarian is checking the Basset's tonsils for infection.

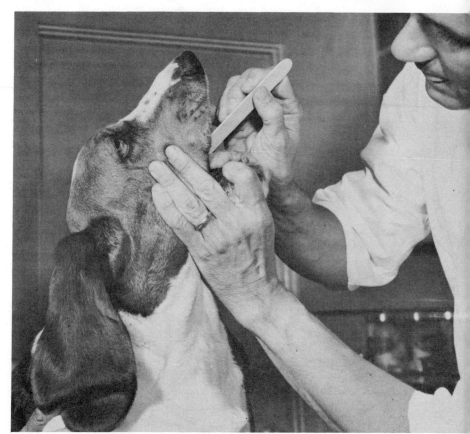

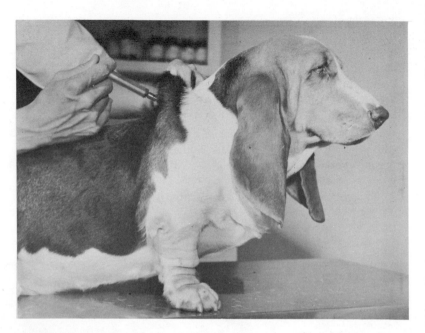

Various methods of immunization against killing
diseases have been developed and are successful.

We see young puppies in the nest, healthy, bright and sturdy; suddenly they begin to vomit, and the next day they are dead of infectious hepatitis—it strikes that quickly. The disease is almost impossible to diagnose correctly, and there is no known treatment that will cure it. Astute authorities claim that if an afflicted dog survives three days after the onslaught of the disease he will, in all probability, completely recover. Prevention is through vaccination. Veterinarian vaccine programs usually combine distemper, hepatitis, and often leptospirosis vaccines.

Rabies

This is the most terrible of diseases, since it knows no bounds. It is transmissible to all kinds of animals and birds, including the superior animal, man. To contract this dread disease, the dog must be bitten by a rabid animal or the rabies virus must enter the body through a broken skin surface. The disease incubation period is governed by the distance of the virus point of entry to the brain. The closer the point of entry is to the brain, the quicker the disease manifests itself. We can be thankful that rabies is not nearly as prevalent as is supposed by the uninformed. Restlessness, excitability, perverted appetite, character reversal, wildness, drowsiness, loss of acuteness of senses, and of feeling in some instances, foaming at the mouth, and many other lesser symptoms come with the onslaught of this disease. Diagnosis by trained persons of a portion of the brain is conceded to be the only way of determining whether an animal died of rabies or of one of the distemper complex diseases. Very little has been done in introducing drugs or specifics that can give satisfaction in combatting this disease; perhaps evaluation of the efficacy of such products is almost impossible with a disease so rare and difficult to diagnose.

In 1948 an avianized modified live virus vaccine was reported, and is being used with success. Quarantine, such as that pursued in England, even of six months' duration, is still not the answer to the rabies question, though it is undeniably effective. It is, however, not proof positive. Recently a dog on arriving in England was held in quarantine for the usual six months. The day before he was to be released to his owners, the attendant noticed that he was acting strangely. He died the next day. Under examination his brain showed typical inclusion bodies, establishing the fact that he had died of rabies. This is a truly dangerous disease that can bring frightful death to animal or man. It should be the duty of every dog owner to protect his dog, himself, his family, and neighbors from even the slight risk that exists of contracting rabies by taking immediate advantage of immunization protection.

FITS

Fits in dogs are symptoms of diseases rather than illness itself. They can be caused by the onslaught of any number of diseases, including worms, distemper, epilepsy, primary encephalitis, poisoning, etc. Running fits can also be traced to dietary deficiencies. The underlying reason for the fits, or convulsions, must be diagnosed by your veterinarian and the cause treated.

DIARRHEA

Diarrhea, which is officially defined as watery movements occurring eight or more times a day, is often a symptom of one of many other diseases. But if, on taking your Basset's temperature, you find there is no fever, it is quite possible the condition has been caused by either a change of diet, of climate or water, or even by a simple intestinal disturbance. A tightening agent such as kaopectate should be given. Water should be withheld and corn syrup, dissolved in boiled milk, substituted to prevent dehydration in the patient. Feed hard-boiled eggs, boiled milk, meat, cheese, boiled white rice, cracker, kibbles, or dog biscuits. Add a tablespoonful of bone ash (not bone meal) to the diet. If the condition is not corrected within two or three days, if there is an excess of blood passed in the stool, or if signs of other illness become manifest, don't delay a trip to your veterinarian.

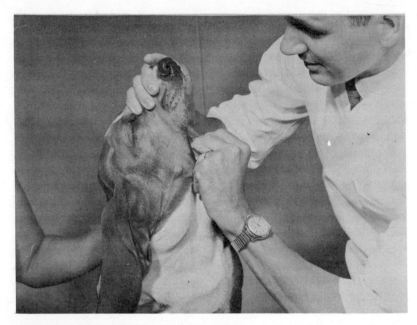

A thorough check by your veterinarian, including
the dog's mouth, can stop diseases in early stages.

CONSTIPATION

If the dog's stool is so hard that it is difficult for him to pass it and he
strains and grunts during the process, then he is obviously constipated. The
cause of constipation is one of diet. Bones and dog biscuits, given abund-
antly, can cause this condition, as can any of the items of diet mentioned
above as treatment for diarrhea. Chronic constipation can result in
hemorrhoids which, if persistent, must be removed by surgery. The cure for
constipation and its accompanying ills is the introduction of laxative food
elements into the diet. Stewed tomatoes, buttermilk, skim milk, whey, bran,
alfalfa meal, and various fruits can be fed and a bland physic given.
Enemas can bring quick relief. Once the condition is rectified, the dog
should be given a good balanced diet, avoiding all types of foods that will
produce constipation.

EYE AILMENTS

The eyes are not only the mirror of the soul, they are also the mirror of
many kinds of disease. Discharge from the eyes is one of the many symptoms warning of most internal virus, parasitic, and bacterial diseases. Of the

ailments affecting the eye itself, the most usual are: glaucoma, which seems to be a hereditary disease; pink eye, a strep infection; cataracts; opacity of the lens in older dogs; corneal opacity, such as follows some cases of infectious hepatitis; and teratoma. Mange, fungus, inturned lids, and growths on the lid are other eye ailments. The wise procedure is to consult your veterinarian for specific treatment.

When the eyes show a discharge from reasons other than those that can be labeled "ailment," such as irritation from dust, wind, or sand, they should be washed with warm water on cotton or a soft cloth. After gently washing the eyes, an ophthalmic ointment combining a mild anesthetic and antiseptic can be utilized. Butyn sulphate, 1 per cent yellow oxide of mercury, and 5 per cent sulphathiazole ointment are all good. Boric acid seems to be falling out of favor as an ophthalmic antiseptic. The liquid discharged by the dog's tear ducts is a better antiseptic, and much cheaper. Basset's eyes, because of the haw being exposed, should be checked and tended frequently.

ANAL GLANDS

If your dog consistently drags his rear parts on the ground or bites this

Checking the ears is an important part of the examination of long-eared dogs.

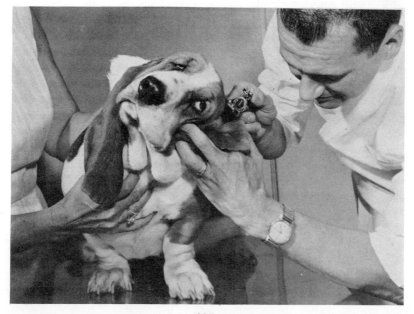

area, the cause is probably impacted anal glands. These glands, which are located on each side of the anus, should be periodically cleared by squeezing. The job is not a nice one, and can be much more effectively done by your veterinarian. Unless these glands are kept reasonably clean, infection can become housed in this site, resulting in the formation of an abscess which will need surgical care. Dogs that get an abundance of exercise seldom need the anal glands attended to.

The many other ailments which your dog is heir to, such as cancer, tumors, rupture, heart disease, fractures, and the results of accidents, etc., must all be diagnosed and tended to by your veterinarian. When you go to your veterinarian with a sick dog, always remember to bring along a sample of his stool for analysis. Many times samples of his urine are needed, too. Your veterinarian is the only one qualified to treat your dog for disease, but protection against disease is, to a great extent, in the hands of the dog's owner. If those hands are capable, a great deal of pain and misery for both dog and owner can be eliminated. Death can be cheated, investment saved, and veterinary bills kept to a minimum. A periodic health check by your veterinarian is a wise investment.

ADMINISTERING MEDICATION

Some people seem to have ten thumbs on each hand when they attempt to give medicine to their dog. They become agitated and approach the task with so little sureness that their mood is communicated to the patient increasing the difficulties presented. Invite calmness and quietness in the patient by emanating these qualities yourself. Speak to the animal in low, easy tones, petting him slowly, quieting him down in preparation. The administration of medicine should be made without fuss and as though it is some quiet and private new game between you and your dog.

At the corner of your dog's mouth there is a lip pocket perfect for the administering of liquid medicine if used correctly. Have the animal sit, then raise his muzzle so that his head is slanted upward looking toward the sky. Slide two fingers in the courner of his mouth where the upper and lower lip edges join, pull gently outward, and you have a pocket between the cheek flesh and the gums. Into this pocket pour the liquid medicine slowly. Keep his head up, and the liquid will run from the pocket into his throat and he will swallow it. Continue this procedure until the complete dose has been given. This will be easier to accomplish if the medicine has been spooned into a small bottle. The bottle neck, inserted into the lip pocket, is tipped, and the contents drained slowly down the dog's throat.

To give pills or capsules, the head of the patient must again be raised with muzzle pointing upward. With one hand, grasp the cheeks of the dog just behind the lip edges where the teeth come together on the inside of the mouth. With the thumb on one side and the fingers on the other, press inward as though squeezing. The lips are pushed against the teeth, and the pressure of your fingers forces the mouth open. The dog will not completely close his mouth, since doing so would cause him to bite his lip. With your other hand, insert the pill in the patient's mouth as far back on the base of the tongue as you can, pushing it back with your second finger. Withdraw your hand quickly, allow the dog to close his mouth, and hold it closed with your hand, but not too tightly. Massage the dog's throat and watch for the

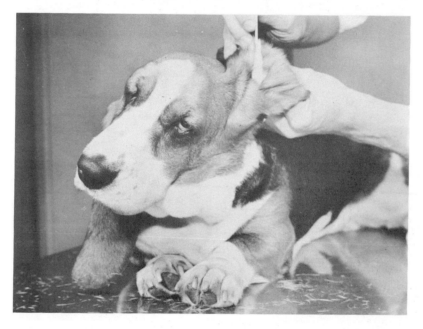

The ears should be kept clean to minimize the
danger of canker or ear mite infection.

tip of his tongue to show between his front teeth, signifying the fact that the capsule or pill has been swallowed.

In taking your dog's temperature, an ordinary rectal thermometer is adequate. It must be first shaken down, then dipped in vaseline and inserted into the rectum for approximately three-quarters of its length. Allow it to remain there for no less than a full minute, restraining the dog from sitting completely during that time. When withdrawn, it should be wiped with a piece of cotton, read, then washed in alcohol—never hot water. The arrow on most thermometers at 98.6 degrees indicates normal human temperature and should be disregarded. Normal temperature for your own dog is 101 degrees; normal puppy temperature varies between $101\frac{1}{2}$ to 102 degrees. Excitement can raise the temperature, so it is best to take a reading only after the dog is calm.

In applying on ophthalmic ointment to the eye, simply pull the lower lid out, squeeze a small amount of ointment into the pocket thus produced, and release the lid. The dog will blink, and the ointment will spread over the eye.

Breaks or bruises should be tended to immediately by your veterinarian.

Should you find it necessary to give your dog an enema, employ an ordinary human-size bag and rubber hose. Simply grease the catheter with vaseline and insert the hose well into the rectum. The bag should be held high for a constant flow of water. Warm soapy water or plain water with a tablespoonful of salt makes an efficient enema.

FIRST AID

Emergencies quite frequently occur which make it necessary for you to care for the dog yourself until veterinary aid is available. Quite often emergency help by the owner can save the dog's life or lessen the chance of permanent injury. A badly injured animal, blinded to all else but abysmal pain, often reverts to the primitive wanting only to be left alone with his misery. Injured, panic-stricken, not recognizing you, he might attempt to bite when you wish to help him. Under the stress of fright and pain, this reaction is normal in animals. A muzzle can easily be slipped over his foreface, or a piece of bandage or strip of cloth can be fashioned into a muzzle by looping it around the dog's muzzle, crossing it under the jaws, and bringing the two ends around in back of the dog's head and tying them. Snap a leash onto his collar as quickly as possible to prevent him from running away and hiding. If it is necessary to lift him, grasp him by the neck, getting as large a handful of skin as you can, as high up on the neck as possible. Hold tight and he won't be able to turn his head far enough around to bite. Lift him by the hold you have on his neck until he is far enough off the ground to enable you to encircle his body with your other arm and support him or carry him.

Every dog owner should have handy a first-aid kit specifically for the use of his dog. It should contain a thermometer, surgical scissors, rolls of three-inch and six-inch bandage, a roll of one-inch adhesive tape, a package of surgical cotton, a jar of vaseline, enema equipment, bulb syringe, ten c.c. hypodermic syringe, flea powder, skin remedy, tweezers, ophthalmic ointment, paregoric, kaopectate, peroxide of hydrogen, merthiolate, army formula foot powder, alcohol, ear remedy, aspirin, milk of magnesia, castor oil, mineral oil, dressing salve.

We have prepared two charts for your reference, one covering general first-aid measures and the other a chart of poisons and antidotes. Remember that, in most instances, these are emergency measures, not specific treatments, and are designed to help you in aiding your dog until you can reach your veterinarian.

FIRST-AID CHART

Emergency	Treatment	Remarks
Accidents	Automobile, Treat for shock. If gums are white, indicates probable internal injury. Wrap bandage tightly around body until it forms a sheath. Keep very quiet until veterinarian comes.	Call veterinarian immediately.
Bee stings	Give paregoric, 1 teaspoonful, or aspirin to ease pain. If in state of shock, treat for same.	Call veterinarian for advice.

Bites (animal)	Tooth wounds—area should be shaved and antiseptic solution flowed into punctures with eye dropper. Iodine, merthiolate, etc., can be used. If badly bitten or ripped, take dog to your veterinarian for treatment.	If superficial wounds become infected after first aid, consult veterinarian.
Bloat	Stomach distends like a balloon. Pierce stomach wall with hollow needle to allow gas to escape. Follow with stimulant—2 cups of coffee. Then treat for shock.	
Burns	Apply strong, strained tea to burned area, followed by covering of vaseline.	Unless burn is very minor, consult veterinarian immediately.
Broken bones	If break involves a limb, fashion splint to keep immobile. If ribs, pelvis, shoulder, or back involved, keep dog from moving until professional help comes.	Call veterinarian immediately.
Choking	If bone, wood, or any foreign object can be seen at back of mouth or throat, remove with fingers. If object can't be removed or is too deeply imbedded or too far back in throat, rush to veterinarian immediately.	
Heat stroke	Quickly immerse the dog in cold water until relief is given. Give cold water enema. Or lay dog flat and pour cold water over him, turn electric fan on him, and continue pouring cold water as it evaporates.	Cold towel pressed against abdomen aids in reducing temp. quickly if quantity of water not available.
Porcupine quills	Tie dog up, hold him between knees, and pull all quills out with pliers. Don't forget tongue and inside of mouth.	See veterinarian to remove quills too deeply imbedded.
Shock	Cover dog with blanket. Administer stimulant (coffee with sugar). Allow him to rest, and soothe with voice and hand.	Alcoholic beverages are NOT a stimulant.
Snake bite	Cut deep X over fang marks. Drop potassium-permanganate into cut. Apply tourniquet above bite if on leg.	Apply first aid only if a veterinarian or a doctor can't be reached.
Cuts	Minor cuts: allow dog to lick and cleanse. If not within his reach, clean cut with peroxide, then apply merthiolate. Severe cuts: apply pressure bandage to stop bleeding—a wad of bandage over wound and bandage wrapped tightly over it. Take to veterinarian.	If cut becomes infected or needs suturing, consult veterinarian. (see TETANUS).
Dislocations	Keep dog quiet and take to veterinarian at once.	

Drowning	Artificial respiration. Lay dog on his side, push with hand on his ribs, release quickly. Repeat every 2 seconds. Treat for shock.	New method of artificial respiration as employed by fire department useful here.
Electric shock	Artificial respiration. Treat for shock.	Call veterinarian immediately.

The important thing to remember when your dog is poisoned is that prompt action is imperative. Administer an emetic immediately. Mix hydrogen peroxide and water in equal parts. Force two to four tablespoonfuls of this mixture down your dog. In a few minutes he will regurgitate his stomach contents. Once this has been accomplished, call your veterinarian. If you know the source of the poison and the container which it came from is handy, you will find the antidote on the label. Your veterinarian will prescribe specific drugs and advise on their use.

The symptoms of poisoning include trembling, panting, intestinal pain, vomiting, slimy secretion from mouth, convulsions, coma. All these symptoms are also prevalent in other illnesses, but if they appear and investigation leads you to believe that they are the result of poisoning, act with dispatch as described before.

POISON	HOUSEHOLD ANTIDOTE
ACIDS	Bicarbonate of soda
ALKALIES	Vinegar or lemon juice
(cleansing agents)	
ARSENIC	Epsom salts
HYDROCYANIC ACID	Dextrose or corn syrup
(wild cherry; laurel leaves)	
LEAD	Epsom salts
(paint pigments)	
PHOSPHORUS	Peroxide of hydrogen
(rat poison)	
MERCURY	Eggs and milk
THEOBROMINE	Phenobarbital
(cooking chocolate)	
THALLIUM	Table salt in water
(bug poisons)	
FOOD POISONING	Peroxide of hydrogen, followed by enema
(garbage, etc.)	
STRYCHNINE	Sedatives. Phenobarbital, Nembutal
DDT	Peroxide and enema

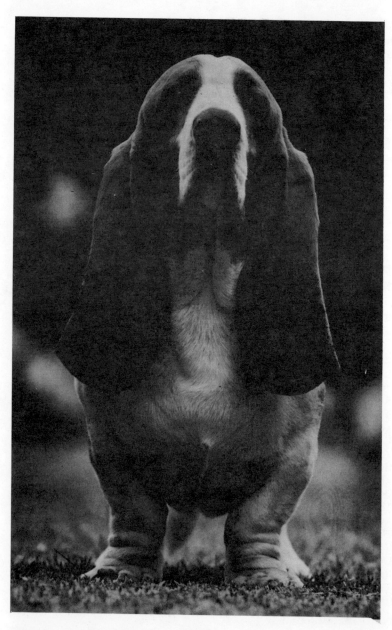

This front view of a fully grown Basset posed
for the judge brings one a sense of the calm,
wise, philosophical character of the breed.

CHAPTER XIV

Standard of the Basset Hound

General Appearance—The Basset Hound possesses in marked degree those characteristics which equip it admirably to follow a trail over and through difficult terrain. It is a short-legged dog, heavier in bone, size considered, than any other breed of dog, and while its movement is deliberate, it is in no sense clumsy. In temperament it is mild, never sharp or timid. It is capable of great endurance in the field and is extreme in its devotion.

Head—The head is large and well proportioned. Its length from occiput to muzzle is greater than the width at the brow. In over-all appearance the head is of medium width. *The skull* is well domed, showing a pronounced occipital protuberance. A broad flat skull is a fault. The length from nose to stop is approximately the length from stop to occiput. The sides are flat and free from cheek bumps. Viewed in profile the top lines of the muzzle and skull are straight and lie in parallel planes, with a moderately defined stop. The skin over the whole of the head is loose, falling in distinct wrinkles over the brow when the head is lowered. A dry head and tight skin are faults. *The muzzle* is deep, heavy, and free from snipiness. *The nose* is darkly pigmented, preferably black, with large wide-open nostrils. A deep liver-colored nose conforming to the coloring of the head is permissible but not desirable. *The teeth* are large, sound, and regular, meeting in either a scissors or an even bite. A bite either overshot or undershot is a serious fault. *The lips* are darkly pigmented and are pendulous, falling squarely in front and, toward the back, in loose hanging flews. *The dewlap* is very pronounced. *The neck* is powerful, of good length, and well arched. *The eyes* are soft, sad, and slightly sunken, showing a prominent haw, and in color are brown, dark brown preferred. A somewhat lighter-colored eye conforming to the general coloring of the dog is acceptable but not desirable. Very light or protruding eyes are faults. *The ears* are extremely long, low set, and when drawn forward, fold well over the end of the nose. They are velvety in texture, hanging in loose folds with the ends curling slightly inward. They are set far back on the head at the base of the skull and, in repose, appear to be set on the neck. A high set or flat ear is a serious fault.

Good Basset front. Legs and feet are correctly set. Chest is good. This type of front is generally referred to as an "English" front.

E·H·H·

Not a good front. Weak in pasterns, feet thin, dewclaws, "Fiddle" or "French" front. Shoulders too narrow. French type Bassets display fronts similar to this but not so exaggerated.

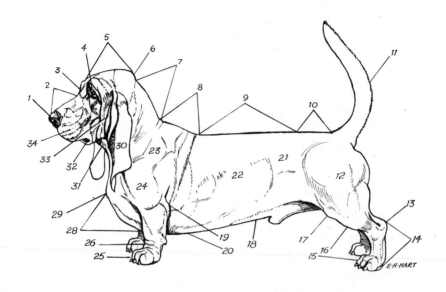

E·H·HART

EXTERNAL STRUCTURE OF THE BASSET

1. Nose 2. Foreface 3. Stop 4. Eye 5. Skull
6. Occiput 7. Neck 8. Withers 9. Back 10. Croup
11. Tail (stern) 12. Thigh 13. Hock joint (point
of hock) 14. Hock 15. Hind feet (toes, digits)
16. Second thigh 17. Stifle 18. Abdomen 19. Elbow
20. Chest 21. Loin 22. Ribs 23. Shoulder blade
(scapula) 24. Upper arm (humerus) 25. Front
feet 26. Pastern 28. Forechest 29. Prosternum
30. Ear (leather) 31. Throat latch 32. Lip corner
33. Cheek 34. Muzzle (lips, flews)

Ch. Santana-Mandeville's Admiral; owners, Mr.
and Mrs. Paul E. Nelson. This fine animal is by
Ch. Santana-Mandeville's Tarzan x Duchess
Chloe Figueras. Show is the Beverly-Riviera K.C.
and the judge is Mrs. A. E. Van Court.

Forequarters—The chest is deep and full with prominent sternum showing clearly in front of the legs. *The shoulders* and elbows are set close against the sides of the chest. The distance from the deepest point of the chest to the ground, while it must be adequate to allow free movement when working in the field, is not to be more than one-third the total height at the withers of an adult Basset. The shoulders are well laid back and powerful. Steepness in shoulder, fiddle fronts, and elbows that are out, are serious faults. *The forelegs* are short, powerful, heavy in bone, with wrinkled skin. Knuckling over of the front legs is a disqualification. *The paw* is massive, very heavy with tough heavy pads, well rounded and with both feet inclined equally a trifle outward, balancing the width of the shoulders. Feet down at the pastern are a serious fault. *The toes* are neither pinched together nor splayed, with the weight of the forepart of the body borne evenly on each. The dewclaws may be removed.

*Body—*The rib structure is long, smooth, and extends well back. The ribs are well sprung, allowing adequate room for heart and lungs. Flat-sidedness and flanged ribs are faults. The topline is straight, level, and free from any tendency to sag or roach, which are faults.

*Hindquarters—*The hindquarters are very full and well rounded, and are

A group of fine young Bassets taking their ease in their kennel quarters.

A very good male Basset show dog. This animal
is a bench show Champion. His quality is evident.

approximately equal to the shoulders in width. They must not appear slack or light in relation to the over-all depth of the body. The dog stands firmly on its hind legs showing a well-let-down stifle with no tendency toward a crouching stance. Viewed from behind, the hind legs are parallel, with the hocks turning neither in nor out. Cowhocks or bowed legs are serious faults. The hind feet point straight ahead. Steep, poorly angulated hindquarters are a serious fault. The dewclaws, if any, may be removed.

Tail—The tail is not to be docked, and is set in continuation of the spine with but slight curvature, and carried gaily in hound fashion. The hair on the underside of the tail is coarse.

Size—The height should not exceed 14 inches. Height over 15 inches at the highest point of the shoulder blades is a disqualification.

Gait—The Basset Hound moves in a smooth, powerful, and effortless manner. Being a scenting dog with short legs, it holds its nose low to the ground. Its gait is absolutely true with perfect co-ordination between the front and hind legs, and it moves in a straight line with hind feet following in line with the front feet, the hocks well bent with no stiffness of action. The front legs do not paddle, weave, or overlap, and the elbows must lie close to the body. Going away, the hind legs are parallel.

Coat—The coat is hard, smooth, and short, with sufficient density to be of use in all weather. The skin is loose and elastic. A distinctly long coat is a disqualification.

211

E·H·HART

FAULTS OF STRUCTURE IN THE BASSET

No. 1
Occiput not strongly enough defined.
Ears slightly lacking in length. Roman
nose. Lack of prosternum. Soft in
pastern. Weak (hare) feet. Too much
tuckup (abdomen). Tendency to rough,
standoff coat. Lack of angulation in rear.
Roached back. Lacks depth of lip
(flews). Too much arch in loin.

Color—Any recognized hound color is acceptable and the distribution of color and markings is of no importance.

DISQUALIFICATIONS

Height of more than 15 inches at the highest point of the shoulder blades. Knuckled over front legs. Distinctly long coat.

Approved January 14, 1964

It might be interesting to compare the present standard with the Basset standard that follows and which was adopted as a yardstick of conformational excellence in the 1880's.

Standard and scale of points of the Basset Hound:

Head	25	Coat	10
Neck and Chest	10	Color	10
Forelegs and feet	15	Size and symmetry	10
Ribs and lion	10		—
Hindquarters and stern	10	Total	100

Head—resembling that of the Bloodhound in shape and dignity of expression, long, rather narrow, and well peaked, with little or no stop. Jaws long, strong, and level; teeth rather small. Nose usually black; but some good ones have had considerable white about theirs. Mouth well flewed. Ears long, large, and soft, hanging like the softest velvet drapery. Eyes are a deep brown, very expressive, rather deeply set, and showing a good deal of haw; expression affectionate, intelligent, and good-humored, though occasionally reflective and melancholy.

Neck and chest—The neck is long, but very powerful, with flews extending nearly to the chest. The chest is well developed, overhanging, and extending to within nearly two inches of the ground.

Forelegs and feet—The shoulders are of great power. Legs very short, and turning inward at the knees; and the feet, which appear to be a mass of joints, considerably bent out.

Ribs and lion—The back and ribs are strongly put together, and the former is of great length.

Hindquarters and stern—The hindquarters are very strong and muscular, the muscles standing out, and clearly defined down to the hocks.

Coat—The skin is soft, and the coat smooth and close, though moderately hard and very weather-resisting in quality, and when the dog is in condition, showing a beautiful natural gloss.

Color—The tri-color, which has a tan head and a black and white body, is much preferred; but they come in all the varieties of white and black-and-tan.

Size and symmetry—Bassets come in all sizes, from nine to twelve inches at shoulder and at from twenty-six to forty-eight pounds in weight and over. The best size is say about eleven or twelve inches at the shoulder and about

FAULTS OF STRUCTURE IN THE BASSET

No. 2

Ears set too high. Lack of stop
indication. Dish faced. Pigeon breasted.
Too high in legs (too much daylight
under dog). Eye not sunken enough.
Lacks somewhat in bone and substance.
Shallow in chest. Mutton withers (flat).
Sway backed. Overbuilt (too high in
croup). Tail too short and carriage is
poor (hound tail should be gay). Ewe
necked (lack of crest indication).

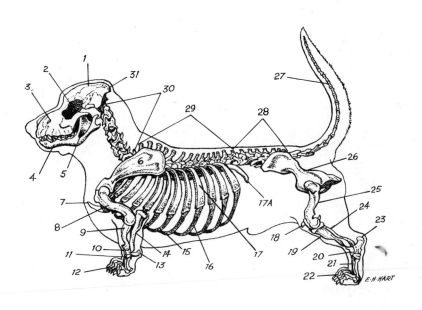

SKELETAL STRUCTURE OF THE BASSET

1. Cranium (skull) 2. Orbital cavity 3. Nasal bone 4. Mandible (jaw bone) 5. Condyle 6. Scapula (shoulder blade) 7. Prosternum 8. Humerus (upper arm) 9. Radius (front forearm bone) 10. Carpus (pastern joint, composed of 7 bones) 11. Metacarpus (pastern, composed of 5 bones) 12. Phalanges (digits or toes) 13. Pisaform (accessory carpal bone) 14. Ulna 15. Sternum (cartilage) 16. Costal cartilage 17. Rib bones 17A. Floating rib (unattached) 18. Patella (knee joint) 19. Tibia (with fibula comprises shank bone) 20. Tarsus (seven bones) 21. Metatarsus (seven bones) 22. Foot 23. Oscalis (point of hock) 24. Fibula 25. Femur (thigh bone) 26. Pelvic girdle 27. Coccygeal vertebra (tail bones) 28. Lumbar vertebra 29. Thoracic vertebra 30. Cervical vertebra 31. Occiput

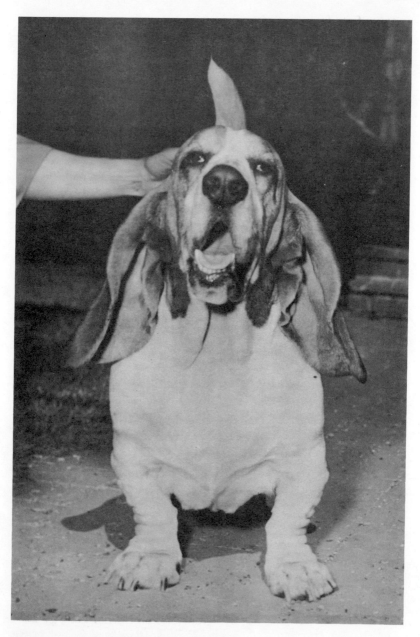

Improper front. This Basset has a good front, but he has not been stacked properly. To correct, the curved lower leg bones should lie closer to the chest and the feet should be aligned.

forty to forty-five pounds in weight. The Basset has more bone in proportion to his size than any other breed, and his symmetry is an important point in his make-up.

A *standard* is a written analysis of a breed. The essence of its combined perfections present to the reader a word picture of a mythical superdog toward which the fanciers must strive. In its entirety, the standard disciplines in selection and rejection toward an ethical center or objective, which is the betterment of the breed.

There have been many who have complained that the standard, as it exists today, is too wordy and unwieldy. Others have suggested that a condensed version be printed for the use of judges, to be used by them in the nature of a freshener prior to judging assignments. Perhaps a better choice of words, in some few instances, would aid in shortening the standard as written, but not to any appreciable extent. It was evidently the purpose of those who were instrumental in fashioning the standard to make it so clear and concise that the reader could, as closely as the written word permits, visualize the ideal. In this design they were eminently successful to the degree that such a document can be successful. Any failure of the reader to know our breed in all its detail does not reflect upon the standard. Rather, it can be blamed upon lack of visual imagination, or faulty interpretation of the written word by the reader. Standards can be too short or too vague, omitting succinct details that, in essence, differentiate the particular breed from all other breeds. A standard is never too long if it is concise and functionally complete. As it exists, it is a worth-while word picture of the breed.

A standard should not be considered rigid and unchangeable. Time brings faults and virtues to a breed which must be recognized and the standard changed in certain particulars to accommodate new values. Since the standard is a yardstick for the show ring and the breeder, evaluation of new trends should be qualified not only by cosmetic application, but by genetic implication as well. Thus, faults which are of an inheritable nature should be penalized far more severely than those which are transient.

The future of the breed is in the hands of the younger generation. Let us hope their skill will match their love for the breed.

CHAPTER XV

The Future of the Basset Hound

What does the future hold for the Basset Hound? We are not seers so we cannot predict the future with any degree of accuracy. We can only review what has gone before and refrain from repeating the mistakes of the past or present and so attempt to find advancement in the time to come. We can advance our own theories in reference to the breed, but they must come from knowledge and objective thought, not arrogance. We must remember that no matter how perfect the dog of the present may be there is always room for improvement in some important aspect of the breed.

The popularity of the Basset Hound has increased manyfold in the last few years. Top wins in large shows have brought recognition to the Basset and curiosity about the breed from dog fanciers. Once these curious ones became more acquainted with the Basset they became confirmed supporters of the breed. From them have come the influx of new breeders and exhibitors that has brought the Basset into the charmed circle of the big ten in A.K.C. registrations. Once the unique qualities of this great, low-to-the-ground hound are savored the swelling ranks of the Basset fancy grows even more.

There has been a relatively steady climb upward toward greater uniformity, beauty, and utility, based on good sense and knowledgeable breeding practice, and the ever increasing interest in the Basset as a gun dog is the sign of a healthy and diversified fancy. To this latter area of endeavor the Basset fancy should give more than lip service. When fanciers of any breed are fortunate enough to find definite utilitarian purpose for their animals it should not be overlooked or given half-hearted support.

The Basset Hound is a sporting dog and we must not forget it. He has the finest scenting ability that can be found in a sporting dog; in fact his ability in this area is so superb it is legendary. He is gifted with a rich and un-parelleled voice which, to the true hound man, is beyond price. Combine these factors with the other grand qualities of this wonderful breed and it is easy to see why his work in the field is so important. Take him out of the field and you rob him of his heritage and his unique gun-dog qualities; his specialized abilities. The Basset can be a pet, a show dog and a gun dog, and in all three areas be superb. He can be only one or two, or a combination of all three of these things and in each area give complete satisfaction to his owner. Truly the Basset Hound has much to offer mankind and particularly that section known as the "dog fancy."

In the final analysis the future of Basset Hound is up to you, the owners and breeders. You must carry the responsibility for molding the future of the breed. Face the future with open minds and tolerance. Learn to understand the many new concepts in care, medicine, and breeding that will be a part of the future and avoid harking back blindly to the incomplete knowledge of the past. It is the job of the breeder to take the tools that new knowledge will fashion and use them well for the betterment of the breed. In the background will always be the knowledge that a smooth-coated, easily kept, hardy sporting dog that can do his job well in home, show ring, and field will always be popular.

In you, the breeder, is vested the power to fashion heredity to mold life in this Basset Hound. You can and, as a breeder, will use this power that creates life and change, that brings special life-forms into being. You can design a pattern of heredity. To do it well, to mold a worthwhile pattern, you must be aware of the power you have and the intelligence to use it well. If the future is to give you what you want for the breed, then you must clear your mind of inaccuracy and absorb truth instead. This then, is the future; a time when yesterday's miracles become today's facts through science and experimentation.

What has gone before has shaped the breed as we know it now. What is done now with the breed will shape its future. It is up to you.

INDEX

A

acquired characteristics, 31
acne, 188
Aerogenes, 99
Afghan, 15
anal glands, 197, 198
A.P.F., 59
Artesian Basset, 21
Artois Dog, 21

B

bacterial diseases, 190-2
Basset a jambes demi-tortues, 21
Basset a jambes droites, 21
Basset a jambes tortues, 21
Basset Grifon, 21
Basset, meaning of, 19
Basset Hound Club, founding in
  England, 25
Basset Hound Club, organizers
  of, 25
Basset Hound Club of America,
  29
bathing, 74-8
Beagle, 22, 26
bicarbonate of soda, 59
Bishop of Liege, 18
Black and Tans, 23
bitch, breeding cycle of, 87
Bloodhound, 18, 22
Blue Gascon, 23

C

calcium in diet, 59
Cameron, Collin, 27
Canis familiaris inostranzewi, 11,
  15
Canis familiaris intermedius, 11
Canis familiaris leineri, 11
Canis familiaris metris-optimae,
  11

Chamberlain, Mr., 27
Chien d' Artois, 21
chromosomes, 34-41
coccidiosis, 184
cod liver oil, 59
competition, classes of, 151-55
Couteult de Conteleu, Count le,
  22
constipation, 196
crooked-legged Basset, 21
Cynegeticus, 15
Cynodictus, 11

D

Dachshund, 19, 23
Darwin, Charles Robert, 31
deficiency diseases, 190
deoxyribonucleic acid, 41
dew claws, 99
diarrhea, 195
distemper, 192-3
DNA, 41
Doberman Pinscher, 19, 25
dog houses, 71-3
Dorsey, Pottinger, 27

E

eczema, 185
Egyptian Greyhound, 15
exercise, 82-83
eye ailments, 196-7

F

false pregnancy, 92
faults, 206, 212, 214
feeding, elements of 55-61
feeding techniques, 62-63
feeding utensils, 63-5
field trials, 167-9
first aid, 200-3
fits, 195

222